XIENTIFIC

XIENTIFIC SOS

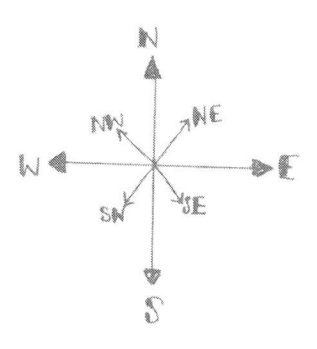

DANIEL PHELPS

ILLUSTRATED BY BETH GIBBS

www.planetpoetry.co.uk

Copyright © 2018 Daniel Phelps

www.xientifica.com / www.planetpoetry.co.uk/xientifica

All rights reserved.

No part of this publication may be reproduced, stored in a retrieval system, or transmitted, in any form or by any means, electronic, mechanical, photocopying, recording, or otherwise, without the prior written permission of the author.

ISBN: 9781980806493

Imprint: Independently published by www.planetpoetry.co.uk

AUTHORS NOTE

For those of you wondering about **'Xientifica'** and how on earth you pronounce it…just think of the 'X' in 'xylophone'. So you might pronounce 'Xientifica' as 'Zi-en-tifica', or perhaps 'Sci-en-tifica'.

If you like Xientifica SOS and want more, please visit www.xientifica.com and www.planetpoetry.co.uk/xientifica the home of planetpoetry® where you can sign up for alerts for new books.

DEDICATION

To you all.

I hope you enjoy Xientifica SOS and it helps in some small way to remind you of the wonders and beauty of the Universe.

ACKNOWLEDGMENTS

Thanks Dad for the science
Thanks Mum for the 'arts'
Thank you family for your patience and support

Thank you Beth for the great artwork.

XIENTIFICA SOS

CONTENTS

1	One Morning in July	Pg 1
2	Candyfloss Clouds	Pg 5
3	Winds of Change	Pg 13
4	Drinking Steam	Pg 20
5	Home?	Pg 28
6	Decisions Decisions	Pg 32
7	Human Scales	Pg 42
8	That Sinking Feeling	Pg 49
9	Carnivorous Cravings	Pg 58
10	Fact or Friction?	Pg 65
11	Two Berry Anna	Pg 72
12	Quentin's Quest	Pg 77
13	Number 1, Palm Trees Court	Pg 80
14	Knock Knock	Pg 88
15	Seeds of Safety	Pg 93
16	Cat-astrophy	Pg 101
17	Over the Edge	Pg 105
18	Dream of the Red Jelly Baby	Pg 111
19	The Mysteries of the Universe	Pg 120
20	Thoughts and Crosses	Pg 125
21	Waiting for Luke	Pg 132
22	School Report	Pg 138

XIENTIFICA SOS

1 ONE MORNING IN JULY

That day, the day that was to change our lives for good, had begun for me just as every other school day had. I had started at Firtrees Primary School, almost seven years ago. It seemed like I'd been there forever. Our game of footy was rudely interrupted by the harsh shrill of the prehistoric brass bell that was still used. That was the signal for registration and hard work. Names were called, 'Yes Miss,' 'Yes Miss,' we replied. We were lined up and we were sat down again in assembly in four and a half minutes flat. Yes, that day was just the same as every other school day. Yes, exactly the same, except that is, for the strange, wry smile on the face of Mr. Carter, our Headteacher. I had never him seen smile before.

He stood facing us, Mr Carter, waiting for the final class to settle. 'I'm waiting,' he said in his teacher's voice, 'until I can hear the hum of that photocopier.' Mr. Carter had said the exact same thing in every assembly that I could remember, and this morning was no exception. The photocopier was in the office next door to the hall, but I had never heard it hum.

The smile, which I had noticed on Mr Carter's face, then began to grow. It was slow at first, but then exploded like a rollercoaster ride. In the twinkling of an eye, Mr. Carter was transformed into the most chilled, most excited looking adult, I had ever seen. He stood there before us, with a magic glint in his eye and a very toothy grin. We had witnessed the first spontaneous personality transplant in history. It was astonishing!

'Ucchmm,' Mr. Carter cleared his throat and straining hard to return to his 'controlled self', began to speak. 'Good morning School. And what a lovely morning it is, if I say so myself. In fact, this is the most lovely and exciting morning that I have ever experienced at Firtrees Primary, since I started here as a young teacher over twenty years ago. This morning I am incredibly proud to be your Headteacher. I have some fantastic news. It gives me enormous pleasure,' he continued, 'to announce that our very own Class 10 have come first...'

At this point Mr Carter started choking and spluttering and the Deputy Head had to step forward to steady him with a fairly firm pat on the back. After a moment or two however, having regained his composure, Mr Carter continued. 'As I was saying, you will all know that our very own Class 10 entered this year's National Schools Science and Engineering Competition and they had to design a new ride for a theme park. The prize for the winning design was for it to be turned into an actual new ride in OrbitaLand in the United States.' He paused and grinned again, 'And as you all know,' he continued, 'the other prize for the winning team, was an all-expenses paid trip to OrbitaLand, in California, and to be the first to try out the new ride. Well,' he said, starting to cough and splutter once again, but finally coming to his conclusion, 'our Class 10… have won!'

At first nobody said anything. I watched Mr Carter standing there, his stupid grin still plastered across his face. I looked around at everyone sitting and standing in the school hall. I looked at the other pupils and the teachers and the reception staff. No one said a word, or moved a muscle. It was then, at that moment, that I could hear the hum of the photocopier for the very first time.

We all knew that winning the competition meant three whole weeks of sun, fun and more fun - the holiday of a lifetime! A theme park with the best and most amazing rides in the whole world. And three weeks of burgers and pancakes and waffles and milkshakes from Heaven - the food of legend! And then to top it all, we would be the first people in the world to ride the newest, most awesome ride in the park - the ride that our class had inspired, the winning idea - the AstroroarUS!

I sat there with all these images racing through my mind and felt this strange feeling bubbling up through me. I knew exactly what it was. It was complete and utter happiness, and it was invading every single cell of my body. I wanted it to stop right there, because if this was all a joke …if this was just a stupid joke by Mr Carter… if it wasn't true …

I couldn't really believe it. It was unthinkable, impossible. This was the ultimate cruel joke. How low could a grown man stoop! I was sure he was about to revert back to the real Mr Carter and say something like, 'Now you know how the winning class from a school in Birmingham must feel now, don't you! If *you* really want to win it next year, then you might want to try a bit harder, Firtrees Primary!' but he didn't.

I looked over at the Deputy Head and the other teachers. They were beginning to clap and big smiles of congratulation danced over their faces. I looked back at Mr. Carter. He could not possibly fake that smile, I thought. He must be telling the truth! Our whole class then went ballistic, jumping up and down screaming, linking arms and stamping feet, completely forgetting where we all were. All the teachers stood applauding us, and the other kids were clapping too - so we just carried on.

That was the beginning. That day back in July was when our lives were launched onto a new and very different course, although we did not know it then. We didn't have to wait long either. The ride had almost been completed, but they had kept it a secret. We would leave the week after school shut for the holidays. The last three weeks of school were a blur. All we could think and talk about was OrbitaLand. Weekends were spent buying all the things we needed; bottles of sun lotion, sunglasses and swimming costumes. The whole world wanted to interview us and take photos of us. We appeared in nine newspapers and we were all over the Web! The weeks dragged on and on and on, but at last, the big day arrived.

2 CANDYFLOSS CLOUDS

'Come on Mr. Close,' called out Mr. Carter sharply across the packed departure area at Heathrow airport. 'Move those legs!' A tall, skinny boy, with short, spikey black hair and glasses, could be seen dashing madly through a crowd of people, half carrying, half dragging a suitcase almost his own size. He skipped nimbly between a middle aged couple and their three young children, but did not notice the folded up pushchair at their feet and crashed to the ground with a thud. The case flung open and clothes tumbled across the floor. Immediately he was on his feet, apologising, adjusting his glasses, and scooping the clothes back into the case as best he could. Then, half shut case skimming the ground behind him, he made the final short dash to the airline check-in-desk and collapsed exhausted.

'We were just about to go without you young man.'

'Sorry Mr. Carter,' he panted, 'Sorry, we got stuck in traffic. Mum's still trying to park.'

'Well I'm glad we didn't have to leave you behind. You're the last. Everyone else has already boarded.'

For some of us, it was the first time that we had flown. I was really lucky, I had a window seat. Looking out, I watched Mr. Carter and my best friend Luke being hurried onto the plane by a lady in a high-vis jacket. Luke was looking slightly embarrassed. The rest of us were all seated together in a group at the rear of the plane. There was a ripple of applause and some cheers as Luke appeared, walked the length of the plane and sat down.

As we soared westward, I looked out at the huge gleaming white wing and into the deep, deep, perfect blue sky above. Candyfloss clouds spread below us like mountains of whipped cream. Each was smooth and silky and perfect. The light was different up here. It sparkled and glistened in a way I'd never seen before. It was amazing. I felt like an eagle swooping through my own kingdom of marble mountains and valleys.

We had been seen off by dozens of mums and dads, aunts and uncles and grandmas and grandads. Even our local T.V. company had turned up! Mum and Dad and Tamara my sister had come to wave goodbye. I reckon they were pretty happy to get some peace for the summer holidays. Along with the twenty-nine of us in our class, there was our form teacher Miss Dawson, Mr. Carter and four other teachers. All in all we were quite a party!

We all loved Miss Dawson. She was ace. She always stuck up for us if we got into trouble with Mr. Carter. She was a brilliant teacher and taught us loads of great stuff. Some days she seemed quite sad though...something to do with her dad I'd heard, but I never knew the details. I was glad she was with us. It was going to be so fun.

Miss Dawson had asked the airline if our group could visit the flight deck and as we were all VIPs, they agreed! We went in, in pairs. I went with Luke, my best friend. We had been best friends for ages and ages. We both liked the same type of music and loved playing football together. Luke was a very quiet boy. He spoke very softly and he was exceedingly polite with grownups. I reckoned this was because he had so much practice saying 'sorry'. He was late for absolutely everything, so he always needed to apologise. As we squeezed into the flight deck we gasped at the million different coloured buttons and levers all around us. Symbols seemed to dance everywhere across electronic-maps. It all looked pretty complicated, like a hundred computer games all in one!

'Hey,' I said, looking out the window, 'we're not moving very fast.' The pilot who was called Robin, gave a little chuckle.

'It looks like that doesn't it, but just you wait until we pass some cloud or another plane, you'll see. We are actually travelling at over 70% of the speed of sound, around 550 miles per hour.'

'It doesn't look like it,' I said. But just then, no sooner as I'd spoken, we whizzed past a whisp of cloud in an instant, revealing our incredible speed.'

'If I threw you out of the window,' said Greg, the co-pilot, with a smile, 'how long do you think you boys would last?'

'Don't know,' I replied.

'About fifteen seconds. Look at that,' he said, pointing to a panel just above his head. 'Minus 53°C. You know, that's much, much colder than your mum's deep freeze. In fact, looking at you two skinny ones, I'd give you ten seconds tops!'

'My ears feel all weird,' said Luke, wriggling a finger in his ear. 'Why's that, is that normal?'

'Well,' said Robin smiling, 'it's because of the air

pressure. You see the air pressure is not so strong when you go up in a plane.'

'What's that then,' I asked, 'the air pressure?'

'Imagine blowing up a balloon,' he said. 'What happens if you keep blowing more and more air into it?'

'It bursts, it pops,' replied Luke.

'That's right. That's the air pushing against the sides of the balloon. We call that 'air pressure.' When you blow up a balloon, the air pressure from the inside is greater than the air pressure from the outside and that's why the balloon inflates.'

'So that's what makes your ears feel odd?' I asked, still not clear.

'Yeah, that's right. When you go up in a plane, the air pressure changes. It isn't as strong as when you are on the ground. And just like a balloon, there's much more push - or pressure - inside your ears, than from the outside and they can go 'pop' too! You see that button there? When I press that, it helps to keep the air pressure in the plane the same as the air pressure from inside in your ears, but it's not perfect. When the pressures are the same, there's no problem, but when the pressures change that's when you can feel it.'

Luke and I chatted with Robin and Greg a while longer and they explained all about how satellites helped pilots to know exactly where they are. Finally, we went back to our seats, heads buzzing with facts and figures. Leaning across me and looking out through the window, Luke as usual was the first to spot the coast of America. The rest of us couldn't see it until shortly afterwards, when our friend Robin announced, 'Ladies and gentlemen, the U.S.A. is just coming into view now!'

Luke was always like that. He was always seeing

things before everyone else. He told me he had learned it from his name 'Luke Close', and that, he said, is exactly what he did! Luke had a favourite poem about 'looking'. He had written it down in my 'Collection of Poems and Riddles' book, which I had started in Year 4. As we looked out at the American coastline, I heard him sing it quietly to himself under his breath.

> **'Look around and you will see**
> **A world of opportunity**
> **Things to do and things to make**
> **And you will learn at such a rate**
> **You won't believe your eyes!**
>
> **So open them - look left and right**
> **And only shut them**
> **When it's night!'**

There was certainly a lot to see right now and I definitely had no intention of shutting my eyes!

Something else you should know about Luke, especially if you ever get to meet him, is that things always seem to go wrong when he's around. I know things go wrong for all of us from time to time, but with Luke, they seem to happen *all* the time. Maybe the bus breaks down, or the car runs out of petrol, the T.V. breaks and so on. Anyway, I just thought you'd better know that.

We left the mighty Atlantic Ocean behind us. I watched it slip away like a dream as we thundered over new landscapes and time zones. We soared high over cities and forests and field after field of all different colours and shapes. God must have had a wonderful time painting with numbers I thought.

We were given our lunch on little trays. Everything was neatly packed into little dishes and packets. In fact, it took me longer to unwrap everything than it did to eat it! Shortly afterwards our trays were collected and then we were instructed to fasten up our seatbelts ready for landing. The air stewards then came around and gave us sweets.

'Suck on these, kid,' said Simon, our smiling air steward. 'That helps make the pressure inside and outside your ears the same.'

'So that's why,' I thought, 'now I know why Mum always takes mints with her when she goes on a plane!'

The plane dived and the trees and buildings below grew larger and larger. Chattering stopped. We sucked hard on our sweets. Ears popped and engines whizzed. Then we were down and stepping out into the heat of the afternoon sun. It was a perfect day. There was not a cloud in the sky. 15:36 read the time on one of the tall, glistening buildings and 30°C. I breathed in a deep, deep breath. 'America at last, OrbitaLand here I come!'

A coach met us and drove us up the coast for about an hour to OrbitaLand and our luxury hotel. We were shown to our rooms and then we all bundled down into the hotel lounge area. We'd been instructed to leave our phones in our rooms for the evening. The teachers had said they wanted our full attention, but we could take them out the next day 'if we really needed to'. Miss Dawson said a few words before introducing Carol to us from the OrbitaLand hotel. Carol who was a tall, slim lady with blond hair in a tight bun and a very squeaky voice, began a short, squeaky presentation about OrbitaLand. 'I hope you've all picked up a pocket map of the park,' she began. 'If not, there's one in your rooms.

You won't need the map just yet though,' she said smiling, as she began to pass us each a VR headset. 'Put them on,' she said, 'Have fun!'

We then, each of us spellbound, experienced in virtual reality the most amazing tour of the world's number one theme park and the wonders that awaited us the next day! One ride we didn't get to see however, was the AstroroarUS! That was not included in the VR tour. It was also sectioned off, Carol told us, in a far corner of the park, and we would have to wait to see it, when it was officially opened in two days' time.

'Now folks,' said Carol, who looked really smart in her blue uniform, 'this evening, you are welcome to explore absolutely anywhere inside the park, but please, don't go outside the boundary. The rides are about to shut now, but don't worry, you're here for two whole weeks, so there's plenty of time to try out everything you want to. You have about an hour to have a wander and to whet your appetite.'

'Oh, one other thing,' said Carol, in an even higher pitched voice than before, 'don't go trying to take a sneak peek at the 'AstroroarUS!', we want to keep that a surprise for you!'

Just then the hotel manager arrived. He had a few words with our teachers before turning to us. He was a short, stocky man. He had dark curly hair, a large round face and a big jolly grin.

'Hi everybody, my name's Dave. Welcome to OrbitaLanddddddddd!' He joked and laughed and answered our thousand questions, and in no time at all, he had us all whooping and cheering and stomping our feet with excitement! Then he raised his hands and waited for silence. In a serious voice, he then asked us all to listen very carefully. The whooping stopped and the buzz of excitement grew quieter and fell silent.

'Well, you guys,' Dave began, 'do you want the gooood news or the baaad news first?' There was a sudden shout of 'bood' and 'gad' and then silence again, as Dave again raised his hand. 'Well, I'm a gonna tell ya the baaad news first. This very morning,' he said lowering his voice, 'we had a hurricane warning.' Luke and I turned to each other and shared a glance of excitement mixed with unease. We weren't at all used to hurricanes in England. 'The good news is though,' continued Dave, as whispers began to fill the room, 'it has turned right around and moooved inland. And,' he went on, 'unlike in your little country, us Americans are used to hurricanes. And I can tell you this, there is nothing to worry your little minds about. If we have to take shelter, we will inform you in gooood time. And now,' he said, with a cheesy smile, 'it's my favourite part of the day, 'Fodder Time'. Enjoy!'

He chuckled to himself and signalled us all into the food hall.

'Mr. Dave,' I called out, 'In England 'fodder' means food for animals.'

'That's right son,' he said, winking at me and smiling. We both laughed as we walked into the food hall where we were greeted by the waft of our 'fodder'. This is what I'd been waiting for, for many weeks! But I had no idea that the next meal I would eat, would be very, very different.

3 WINDS OF CHANGE

'Let's go and explore,' said Luke excitedly, as soon as we had finished a huge plate of fried chicken, fries, 'slaw' and salad.

'Luke!' I replied, looking him straight in the eyes, and that was enough. He knew exactly what I meant.

'Okay, okay. As soon as you've had your seconds then,' he said impatiently. I was usually the impatient one. But food, well, I liked food, especially this food.

Seconds demolished, five friends, Luke, Quentin, Anna, Aisha and myself, set off to explore the delights of OrbitaLand. I don't remember too much about it though. At the time, it seemed like we were in a kaleidoscope of rides and sounds and colours and smells. Excitement was pulsing through me as we skipped through the winding paths of the tropical park gazing, just gazing, with mouths open wide. I looked around at rides of all descriptions. Up and down, round and round, inside out and outside in! Some looked as though they had come straight from NASA!

However, as I just mentioned, I don't remember all I

should. This is because the events that greeted us next, make it all seem, well…very small and dull. Our eyes and our brains were about to be opened. An adventure a million miles from Firtrees Primary School was creeping fast and secretly towards us. We just didn't know it.

'This way,' I called, turning my map around, 'The beach is that way, behind 'Cloudskimmer'. The others followed. 'Cloudskimmer' was the highest ride in the whole World. It had only been finished two months ago, but every kid on Earth knew about it. It had been shut all day because of the hurricane warning but would be open at nine o'clock the following day. 'Wow, just look at that,' gasped Luke, as we passed underneath. I looked and stared and gulped. The thing was incredible - it was a giant. Its silver structure glistened breathtakingly in the evening sun. My stomach rolled over.

'Errrgh look QUICK! IT'S FALLING!' I cried.

'No it's not, you wally,' said Anna. 'It's just the clouds moving past it. They make it look like it's falling.'

'Oh yeah, you're right,' I said relieved and blamed my panic on the jetlag.

'Come on you guys,' urged Quentin, 'Let's check out that beach.'

'Good idea,' I said, beginning to feel very, very queasy. With the jetlag and 'Cloudskimmer', I felt I could do with some sea-air. We turned a corner and there in front of us was the beach and the sea beyond. For me, this looked as though it would be my favourite part of the park. Although there were no big rides on the beach, I could see dozens of different watersports - jet-skiing, surfing, sailing, water-skiing, parasailing … the choice was huge. As we strolled along the front I made a shopping list in my mind of what I was going to try out the next day.

In our excitement, we hadn't noticed that the weather had been changing dramatically. The blue skies were blackening fast and the wind was picking up. We only then noticed that there was no longer anyone else around. The park seemed pretty much deserted apart from a few OrbitaLand staff rushing here and there and pulling down shutters frantically. Then we felt the first drops of rain. And then almost immediately they were coming down thick and fast. I had never known a sky change so rapidly. We looked around anxiously for some shelter. There were no suitable trees to duck under, nor any buildings that seemed open anywhere nearby.

'There,' shouted Luke pointing.' Fifty metres away however, across the beach, was a small, rickety looking wooden hut or boathouse. So we ran for that. We covered our heads from the rain as we ran. Rain that was now turning into hail - big painful hail! Already drenched and bruised we reached the hut. We yanked open the wooden doors which luckily for us, were unlocked. We peered into the gloomy hut and searched for a light, but there wasn't one. It was just a small wooden hut, with nothing in it, apart from a small rowing boat covered by a thick tarpaulin. There was one other small detail, this small wooden hut, had a wooden roof that was peppered with large ~~wooden~~ holes.

Five soggy children clambered quickly into the boat and into the blackness under the tarpaulin. A bundle of arms, legs and rucksacks wriggled blindly into some sort of order. And there we sat, cramped and cold, whilst the storm around us stepped up another gear.

'Ugh, is that your feet Anna?' joked Luke, as the stench of fish and mouldy canvas stormed our nasal passages.

'Get lost barnacle brain.' She giggled, and we all

laughed nervously.

Anna always gave as good as she got. She was a very determined girl and set her sights on being a 'Doctor of the Mind', as she put it. I thought she would make a good doctor. She was always calm and patient and was good at thinking problems through in a logical way.

Outside however, it wasn't at all calm. The force of the wind buffeted the small hut with increasing strength. Hail smashed down on our feeble shelter like a million angry fists. I heard the wind tear under the gaps in the wooden walls and shake our little boat violently. Howling gusts, cracking planks, flapping canvas, screaming ...screaming. I squeezed my hands over my ears to cut it all out, but the noise wouldn't stop. It just grew louder.

Our boat continued to rock and we could hear our feeble shelter disintegrating around us. Then all of a sudden, I sensed the strangest and most frightening feeling … we were moving! We were actually moving and we weren't moving slowly! We were being hurled and flung like a sheet of newspaper across the sands by a mighty gust of wind. Us in the boat, in the hut - what was left of it. We clung to each other terrified. The noise of the hurricane was now deafening. For this is surely what it was - the hurricane that we had been told had moved inland!!

We hung on to each other in the dark as we were tossed this way and that. Have you ever seen a mouse being thrown around by a cat? Well, that's what it was like. We were the mouse and the wind was the cat. We were completely at the mercy of the power of nature. However, a moment later, things got even more terrifying. I felt a very strange sensation. We were still moving. There was no doubt about that. However this was different. I dared myself to lift the tarpaulin a fraction and peep out. What I saw I had already guessed. We were out at sea - far out at sea! The hut had gone, the beach was disappearing rapidly and our little boat was being skimmed across huge waves, like a flat stone. I ducked back under the canvas, pulling it tightly down over my head. It was too noisy to say anything to the others. They wouldn't hear me. They knew anyway. We could all feel the spray of the waves as well as the rain crashing on top of us, as our boat lurched violently here and there. This was the end of us for sure. So much for the 'holiday of a lifetime'. It was the last holiday of our lifetime! Soon we would all be flung helpless into the belly of this angry sea and swallowed whole - rucksacks and all.

But that didn't happen. Instead, hours and hours went by, and we were still in the boat, dazed, sick and badly bruised. And then suddenly, all became calm. An eerie stillness rose up around us. It was deathly quiet. Slowly we all poked our heads out from under the tarpaulin and gazed about in disbelief. We were surrounded by sea. Above us was blue sky. It was already morning! We were in the middle of the ocean in a small beaten up boat, bruised and shaken, but still alive! We looked around us. There was blue in all directions, nothing but blue, beautiful, calm, soothing blue.

We then soon became aware of the sun's heat. It was still low in the sky, but it was already strong. It was going to be a hot day. I instinctively reached into my pocket for my mobile phone – all of us did, at once. And we all realised at once that all our phones were still in our main luggage where we had been told to put them. 'Well,' piped up Aisha, 'in case we're not picked up for a while, we had better keep that water,' she said, pointing out the many small pools of water that were caught up between the creases of the canvas. 'Just in case,' she added, 'and also, we would be sensible to keep out of this hot sun as best we can.'

How Aisha was able to think clearly like that after what we had just gone through, was a mystery to me. The rest of us were still stunned and silent. We all juggled positions so that we were sitting in a kind of circle, each with our back to the edge of the boat. In between us was the crumpled tarpaulin sheet, which held the water.

'I expect they're looking for us now,' said Aisha, breaking the silence again. 'We'll be picked up shortly I'm sure.' That was Aisha, always optimistic, bubbly and forward thinking. Aisha wanted to be an actress. She always had done since she was a toddler, her mum had told me once.

'Yer know what I told her a few years back?' she had said to me. 'Yer five years old young lady, and ye still think you can make a career in Ollywood! Yer fooling yerself girl. It'll take a lot more than yer pretty dark eyes and ye curly locks, I can tell ya. You should be spending more time on ye school work and less time in that make believe world of yers!' Poor Aisha, no wonder she needed to be positive and have a good imagination - with a mum like that!

Like Luke, Aisha had also written a favourite poem in my book. This is it:

'Now some days your life seems a pile of gloom
When it's dark and your heart is not singing its tune
When the flowers are black and the air is like lead
And you'd much rather spend the next two years in bed.

But something that you need to keep in your mind
Is the world can be cruel but can also be kind

And the mist that is there at the start of the day
By the heat of the sun can be soon put away.

So be like the sun as it shines every day
Even if there are dark clouds in the way
If you rise and you smile, and you hold your head high
You will help both yourself and others who cry.'

'I bet they won't be long now,' said Aisha smiling. She was wrong.

4 DRINKING STEAM

By evening we had each finished the cans of Coke that we had in our rucksacks. I looked down at the water trapped on the canvas tarpaulin. Then slowly, I bent down to drink.

'Yuck.' I spat it out as soon as it had touched my lips. 'Seawater, *not* rainwater!' It must have been from the waves splashing over us I thought. Slowly it dawned on me. We were thirsty and the only water we had left - we couldn't drink. It was getting dark and it was getting cold. A sickly fear started to creep over me. I couldn't stop it.

'We're going to die,' I blurted out, 'we're gonna die of thirst, or freeze to death – or both! What we gonna do?' Silence followed and then more silence. 'Somebody say *something*!' I shouted eventually. But no one said anything. Everyone was thinking the same as me.

Eventually, Luke raised a weary arm and pointed at the tarpaulin in front of him. 'I've been watching those tiny puddles all day,' he said. 'You know, I was sure they were getting smaller. And look, I was right. Some have completely disappeared. They've vanished into thin air!'

'I once saw a programme about that,' said Anna sleepily, covering a yawn with her hand. 'Puddles in the sun dry up because the water has *evaporated*. You know, like the milk,' she added with a forced grin.

'Yeah, you're right,' said Luke. I remember last summer, I went out in our garden really early in the morning, when the grass was still wet. When the sun got to it, steam came off the grass, like out of a kettle. It didn't take long before the grass was completely dry.

'But what's that left behind?' asked Luke, peering down puzzled at where there was once a puddle. He wiped a finger slowly across the white patches that had appeared in and around the creases of the tarpaulin. 'They're like little crystals,' he cried out.

'I know what that is,' said Quentin. 'It's sea salt. We have it on our food at home.' He dabbed a dry tongue with his finger then pressed it into the powdery white crystals. Carefully, very carefully, he licked the tiniest bit with his tongue. 'Yep,' he said, screwing up his face and spitting overboard. 'Salt. Great. Now all we need is fish and chips and a dash of vinegar!'

We all fell silent again, but not for long. Suddenly Anna sat bolt upright. She brushed her brown hair away from her sparkling eyes. Her face was alight. We could almost see her thoughts zipping around inside her head, like a ball in a pinball machine. This was her 'supersonic thinking' that we all knew and loved.

'But if,' she began softly, 'if the salt stays behind, then what about the water that comes off?'

'What about it?' we all replied unimpressed.

'We could drink it! We could drink it!' she chanted. 'That's what. Can't you see? If it has lost its salt, it should be *okay* to drink!'

'Yes she's right,' said Quentin perking up. But then

another thought made his face drop again. 'But we can't drink steam Anna...'

'Yes we can,' she said, butting in before he had even finished speaking. 'We can drink steam. Well sort of... listen,' she said almost secretively. 'I remember once when Mum was making a cup of tea, I held a metal tray above the steam as it came out of the kettle. When the steam hit the tray, it turned back into water drops. Mum said the steam con...cond...something...like that other milk you can get in tins. You know, it's really *sweet*. You know um, *condensed*, that's it, *condensed!* That means it turns back into water.'

So that was that. Together we had cracked it! We had enough water around us for a million years. All we needed to do was to heat up the salty seawater. The water would then come off, or 'evaporate', as steam. Then we just had to cool the steam - so that it turned back into water - and collect it. But how could we do that? What could we use? We emptied out our pockets and rucksacks and laid out all we had in front of us. We stared at the pile. Four empty Coke cans, a couple of biros, an empty lunch box, my notepad, five maps of OrbitaLand, some chewing gum and a few coins.

Well, I expect *you,* who's reading this, are sitting in your comfy chair, probably with a nice cool lemonade or something. So I suspect that you haven't a clue how you would make fresh water from salty seawater. I bet we couldn't have either, if we had been in your situation. However, when you're desperate, when you need something really, really badly, like we did then, it's amazing what your brain can do.

Well, we stared at that pile of bits and bobs in front of us for a long time. Then Anna slowly leaned forward and picked up two of the empty cans and a biro.

'Quentin, would you make a little hole in the side of each can for me, here and here. One high up on this can, and on this other one, slightly lower down. Use that nail there,' she said, pointing at a small nail lying near to Quentin's foot.

'No problem,' he said and he set to work. We then watched Anna dismantle the biro. She took out the inside to give her the empty plastic tube. Then, leaning over the side of the boat, she scooped some seawater up into the first can; the one with the highest hole in it. She then joined the two cans together by lodging the biro tube between the holes that Quentin had made. She took some chewing gum, softened it in her mouth and used it to seal the edges of the holes around the biro. She blocked the holes on top of the cans by placing a coin over each. Next she sealed them - again with chewing gum. The rest of us looked on puzzled, trying to figure out how it was all going to work.

'Right,' she said at last, 'this is how it's going to work. The water in this can will get heated up by the hot sun. Some of it will turn into steam. The steam will travel along the biro-tube into the empty can. We'll keep this second can cold, so when the steam enters it, it will turn back or 'condense' into water. The salt will stay here in the first can!' She finished triumphantly and stared at us breathless.

① HEAT

② EVAPORATION   ③ CONDENSATION

Next she took the sandwich-box and scooped some more water into it. That,' she said, 'will be like a cold bath for the empty can. It will keep it cool so the water doesn't evaporate back again. We'll cover it as well, so the sun doesn't get to it.'

Finally the 'salt-separator' was ready for action. There was however one major problem. For the water to evaporate quickly, it had to be hot. By the time Anna had constructed the 'salt-separator', the sun had virtually disappeared. And within a very short while, the pink ball had been swallowed up whole by the horizon. It all seemed to happen much more rapidly than back home. Quentin said this was because we were now much closer to the equator. In any case, fresh water would have to wait until tomorrow.

All was now silent apart from the gentle slurping of the waves under our boat. Everything seemed so big and we seemed so small. Sweeping above us we could clearly see the dusty band of the Milky Way. To the east, a yellow half-moon was beginning to climb. Although it was quite mild and there was very little wind, we felt cold and we huddled together for warmth and comfort.

In the darkness, every second felt like an eternity. Each minute stretched out like chewing gum stretched between mouth and fingers. Time seemed stuck. At some point however, we did all fall asleep and slept soundly under the stars. And whilst we slept, time must have unstuck itself. For when we awoke again, the sun had already risen and was demanding a new day.

Anna's water plan could now begin. The sun was rapidly heating up. Soon it would be scorching again. Just the thought of it was terrible. I swallowed, my mouth was so dry and tight and my stomach groaned. I was so pleased I had stuffed down two platefuls of chicken and fries at the hotel. In hope, I scanned the horizon. There was still no hint of a boat or plane coming to rescue us.

The only thing that cheered us up a bit was a fantastic idea that Luke came up with. Luke is long-sighted. That means he can only see clearly things that are far away. His glasses help to focus light for him. This helps him see things close by. Luke suggested using his glasses to focus the sun's heat onto the can with the water in it. This would heat up the water a bit quicker and speed up the evaporation. It was a *blinding* idea I thought, especially for Luke, as he had to donate his glasses to the cause!

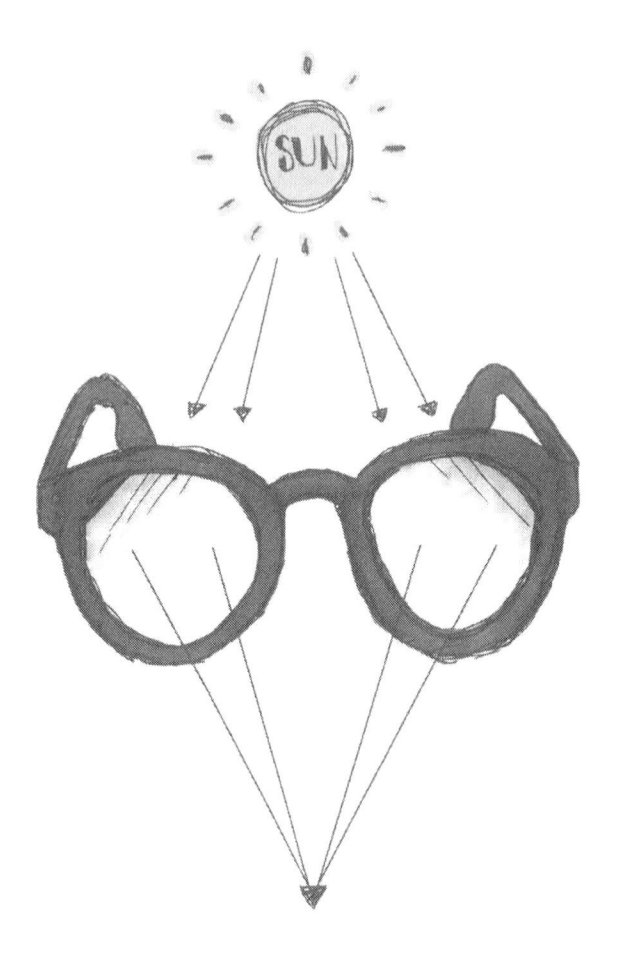

The day dragged on sluggishly. How slow time goes when you're bored or in pain. I imagined if we'd been enjoying ourselves at OrbitaLand, two weeks would have already sped by. Funny that, how time can stretch and squash like a spring. I wished the stretching and the squashing were the other way around. That way the fun days would last forever and ever and the horrible ones would simply fly by.

'How's it going Anna?' piped up Aisha encouragingly.' Anna lifted the collecting can and shook it.

'Nah, nothing yet,' she replied.

'*Nothing yet*!' cursed Luke. 'I've been blind for half a day for 'Nothing yet!" His words seemed to write themselves in big letters across the sky. 'Sorry Anna. I didn't mean to snap. It's just...,' he paused, 'well... I'm frightened.'

'Why are there no boats?' I croaked, to cover up Luke's words. My face burned red and my mouth begged for liquid. I had a good idea now how it might feel to eat a packet of flour! I made up my mind right then, that if by a miracle we did survive, that I would never, ever, leave a tap dripping, or waste a single drop of water *ever* again.

Once more the sun finally decided to drop from its throne in the sky. We had come to another evening. 'I'll take a look,' whispered Anna hoarsely. She shook the can once more and this time, there was water! But not much - a few drops each at the most - barely enough for one, let alone five of us! The idea had seemed good in theory, but it hadn't worked that well in practice...We passed around the can, sipped it gently, and somehow fell into a half-sleep. This was the end for us. We knew it. But no-one said it.

5 HOME?

A huge jolt and a sound like a plane taking off, woke us suddenly from our restless dreams. We rubbed our eyes. We were still alive! And to our joy and amazement we could see land! Our boat had hit a rock (which we later found to be a coral reef). This was both good and bad. The 'good' - we were near land. The 'bad' – the hull of our boat had been sliced in two. The five of us soon found ourselves sitting in a foot of water which was rising fast. In a flash, forgetting our weary bodies, we grabbed our few belongings and began to swim to the shore. Behind us our wooden boat dropped swiftly downward and disappeared from view. The tarpaulin was left bobbing up and down on the water like a large carpet of seaweed. Soon it too was washed up on the sand beside us.

We lay there on the sand, in our soaked tee-shirts and shorts, once more aware of our exhaustion and thirst. None of us could move. It was another scorching day. The yellow ball above was drying us out fast and we could feel it attacking our already red and blistering skin.

'Let's go,' I croaked, 'or we will soon turn into dried prunes. Let's find help and let the police know that we're here.' There was nobody around however and this seemed quite strange for such a lovely beach. Come to think of it, there were no signs of human life at all; no boats, no buildings, not even any rubbish!

'Follow me,' said Quentin, marching up the beach with a renewed energy. He then disappeared into a jungle of bushes and palm trees. Off he went with his mop of mousy blond hair, which always looked as if someone had just rubbed it briskly with a towel. Wearily, the rest of us hauled ourselves up and followed him across the sands and into the bushes. It was hard work, but we forced ourselves on. I was sure that we would soon come across a path or a road, but there was none. For about an hour, we all stumbled on through dense foliage. Eventually the trees thinned out and we found ourselves at the foot of a steep rocky climb. And there, we found our treasure! A small stream trickled merrily down between the rocks and into a tiny rivulet at the bottom. We raced over to it and threw our mouths to the ground and into the life-saving water. We guzzled and guzzled, mouthfuls upon mouthfuls of the most wonderful, cool and refreshing liquid, ever discovered by mankind. Only when we were bloated and the cold mountain water had numbed our lips, did we stop. We sat back on the rocks and looked around us and then up at the steep climb in front of us.

'Come on we can do it,' said Aisha. 'And from the top, I bet we'll be able to see which way to go.'

So after a long rest we began to climb. At first it wasn't too difficult, but gradually it became steeper and steeper. Breathing deeply, we sucked oxygen desperately into our lungs. As we climbed higher, the rocks grew larger, and the green grass was replaced by heather and shingle. Quentin, who was very athletic and much fitter than the rest of us, reached the summit first. He was the first to see. I was second. We stood next to each other and gazed around us. I looked out at the beach where we had landed. Then I slowly turned around in a full circle - a whole 360 degrees. We looked at each other in silence, as we took in what we saw. My heart sank.

There was sea all around. We were on an island and by the looks of it, a deserted island. The only sign of life was the sound of Luke trying to catch his breath below us. All about us, all we could see was sea - glorious deep blue sea. Luke, Anna and Aisha soon joined us and we stood there together for a long while. In silence, we looked out at the stunning, but disturbing view before us.

'Well,' I said at last, breaking the silence in two, 'I'm hungry…and there's no use thinking the worst. Let's get back to the beach and try and find some food.' So back down we went, each with our own thoughts, back towards the beach where we had landed. On our way there however, we stumbled across a banana tree crammed full of fruit. With huge relief we gorged ourselves on five or six bananas *each*! Wow, did they taste good. The finest water and now the tastiest bananas ever! All stuffed, we snoozed under the banana trees. Then, eventually, feeling revived, we set off back to the beach, rucksacks crammed with even more bananas!

It was almost dusk when we arrived back at the landing site. We were so tired that we slept easily on the soft sand. The large boat tarpaulin was our only protection.

'I wonder how many grains of sand there are in the world?' asked Quentin curiously, as he slipped into dreamland.

'Lots,' I whispered, as I joined him and the others, in

that secret world of make-believe.

6 DECISIONS DECISIONS

'Cock a doodle doooooeee,' yelled Quentin at the top of his voice. 'Time to get up. Things to do. People to meet,' he chirped cheerily. I forced open one eye and gazed up. Above me was a blurred image of Quentin. I looked up sleepily into his sunburned face with its nose that bent slightly to the left. Quentin joked it had been broken in a boxing contest. However, as Quentin was such a terrible practical joker, I guessed he had once chosen the wrong person to joke with!

At first I was a little confused, but my sandy pillow soon reminded me where I was. I sat up and looked out at the vast ocean in front of me. Then I looked around at the others. They were already awake. I then remembered. Nobody on Earth knew we were here. We were last seen perhaps hundreds of miles away in a theme park and nobody even knew that we were still alive! Anna then spoke.

'Listen,' she said calmly, taking a deep breath. 'We must make some plans. We've got to organise ourselves, just in case we're not found for a while. I think we should do things just like back home. We should work during the week and have some rest and fun at the weekend. What's the day today?'

None of us knew. We didn't have our phones, nobody was wearing a watch, and the days in our boat all seemed like a blur to us now. 'Right,' said Anna, 'We'll have a vote. And that's what we did. And Wednesday won.

Quentin ran off down to the shore. He found a sharp stone and carved 'Wednesday 29th July' on the trunk of a nearby palm tree. Then underneath he wrote, 'I' to show we had been on the island one day.

'By keeping a tally chart like this,' he said, 'we can see just how long we have been here. Every time we get to five, we can put a line through like this,' he explained, drawing his finger through the sand.

'Good,' said Anna, 'Now I think we should have a meeting every morning. You know, a bit like assembly. That way we can share ideas and make plans. Let's go and wash, find some fruit and have our first meeting in about half an hour.' We did as she suggested. Very soon we were sitting in a circle and cracking open some coconuts we had discovered, on the rocks. It wasn't easy at first, but soon we got the hang of it and before long we were guzzling the sweet milk inside. Coconuts are 'top fodder'; food and drink, all in one! Aisha had also found some mangoes that tasted heavenly. It was the best breakfast I'd ever tasted. 'And very good for you too, fresh fruit,' I imagined my mum saying. 'Lots of vitamins and minerals'. I suddenly missed my mum badly, but I pushed her out of my mind, before I started to well up.

When we had finished, we decided that the very first thing we should do was to go and explore the island properly. Later on we could think about building ourselves some proper shelter. It was still early in the morning and not too hot, so we decided to set off straight away. We walked clockwise along the beach. I made up my mind to take notes in my notepad so that later I could sketch a proper map of the island. After several attempts this was my final sketch…

The sand was a glorious white colour and was wonderfully fine. We took off our trainers and it felt so good having the powdery sand under our bare feet. We felt better now that we were doing something positive. To be honest, you really couldn't feel too unhappy in a paradise like this. As we walked, we paddled in the glittering breakwater. Now and then we bent down to try to catch one of the hundreds of minute fish that kept nipping at our ankles. They were always far too quick for us. Each time they managed to dart away from our clumsy fingers. Imagine, to them they must have seemed like giant claws coming out of the sky!

It didn't take long of course before Quentin had started a water fight. He splashed me. I splashed Aisha. She splashed Luke, and that was it. It was all against all. Arms and legs beat the water madly into a frenzy of spray and bubbles. None of us minded because the water was warm like a bath. We soon however slumped exhausted to the ground, the water covering our bodies and our five heads sticking out.

We noticed that we had arrived at a kind of bay, where the water was shallow and was particularly warm. This led back into a river which we followed inland, through the trees for perhaps a mile. We then made an amazing discovery. First we heard it. Then we gazed up in wonderment at the most beautiful waterfall, pouring majestically into a dazzling blue lagoon. Encircling the lagoon was a magnificent canopy of tropical plants. The spray of the waterfall sparkled in the sun like a million sparks and split the light up into tiny rainbows, which hovered over the rocks like angels.

'*Why* do you get those rainbows?' I asked gazing into the tumbling waters.

'Well I'm glad you asked that one,' said Anna, 'cos I've always wanted to know that.'

'I kinda know,' said Aisha, 'but I'm not sure if I can explain it.'

'Go on, have a go Aisha,' urged Anna.

'Okay,' she sighed reluctantly, screwing up her face as she thought.

'The white light from the sun', she began, 'is made up of all the colours of the rainbow: red, orange, yellow, green, blue, indigo and violet. I remember that from '*Run*

Or You Get Boiled In Veg.' My brother made that up! Anyway,' she continued, 'the water drops split up the sunlight into its different parts, its different colours. And that's it really. We see all the different parts - all the colours.'

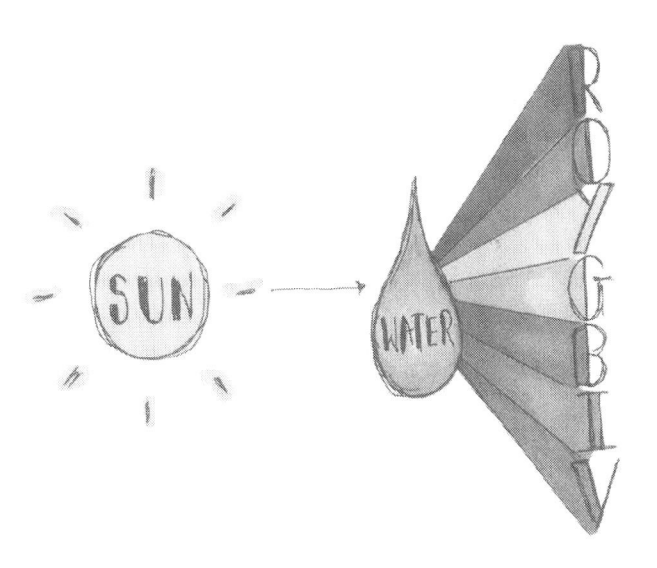

We walked around the lagoon and over to the foot of the waterfall. Aisha loved climbing, and she was soon scrambling up the fern sprinkled rocks beside the tumbling waters. 'Come on you lot,' she called out, 'it's easy.' We followed her over the rocks and up the edge of the falls. When we looked up again however, she had vanished. She had just gone, without a trace.

'Aisha, Aisha,' we yelled. 'Aisha where are you?' We kept calling out, but all we could hear was the gushing waters smashing down into the lagoon below. If she had fallen, surely we would have seen her and heard her scream? And then suddenly she appeared again, out of nowhere. Relieved, we clambered up onto the ledge where she was standing. Laughing and signalling to us, she led us right *behind* the waterfall and into a space from where we could look back through the tumbling spray, with hardly a drop touching us.

She then beckoned us deeper into the blackness of the cave. Deeper and deeper we crept. We huddled together as we inched our way forward, our eyes adjusting to the darkness. The cave breathed a dank, chilly breath that made us cough. I stroked the cold rock wall with my fingertips to guide me. It was smooth where water had worn it down. As we crept on, the noise of the waterfall softened until we could no longer hear it.

Strangely the cave was not entirely dark. There was a faint glow that came from deep within. As we moved deeper inward, the glow grew brighter and brighter and we could now see where it was coming from. High up in the roof of the cave, narrow shafts of light reached down like fingers into the darkness. The light hit the walls which seemed to sparkle and light up themselves. In places I saw small clumps of mossy plants that had found just enough light to grow. Aisha egged us on, 'Come on, let's see where this takes us.'

We followed her and finally came to the far end of the cave. Here the sunlight also squeezed itself through the rock ceiling above. It landed on the cave floor next to us, revealing two holes. Kneeling beside them, we peered sheepishly down. Below us, was another cave. When we crouched down lower, we could see that it was much larger than the one we were standing in. The light above us was shafting through the holes and illuminating this cave too. It flickered and danced on the rock walls and on the cave floor below. As we looked more carefully however, we could see there was something odd about the floor. It seemed to move. It wasn't solid. At first we couldn't work out what it was. Then we realised. It was alive...it was wriggling and writhing around. 'I know what they are,' whispered Anna. 'They're eels...electric eels!' I recognised them too. Anna was right. Below us was a pool of electric eels - thousands of them - and they were squirming around like maggots in a tin.

'Look there,' whispered Luke, as we stood up. He was pointing to the rock wall directly in front of us. Carved unmistakably into the dark rock was an arrow pointing straight downward - at the two holes! We froze.

'My goodness,' I shuddered, 'somebody else is on the island, or has been here at some time!' Suddenly frightened, we turned and stumbled back towards the cave entrance. But as we made our way back, instead of growing brighter, the light in the cave seemed to grow dimmer and dimmer. We soon found ourselves crawling along on all fours in total darkness. Eventually and with great relief, we heard the sound of the crashing waters of the falls once again. Something was not right however. Something was very, very wrong. The waterfall was directly in front of us. By the sound of it, it was no more than a metre away. But unlike before, when we came into the cave, we couldn't see it. Beyond it there was no longer daylight, but almost total darkness! With racing pulses we gingerly edged our way out on to the outside edge and clung to each other trembling. We had been in that cave no more than half an hour and it had been bright sunshine when we had gone in. In fact it couldn't have even been midday. Had the sun died? Had the world ended? Had we gone blind?

'Why can't we see anything?' muttered Quentin. 'And listen, the birds, you can't hear them. They've stopped singing.'

'What's going on?' I whispered.

Next to me, Aisha suddenly began to whistle. And soon, don't ask me why, but we were all joining in with her and whistling away. There we were, standing petrified on a narrow ledge half way up a waterfall, all whistling the National Anthem. What's more, we were on an island that might not be as deserted as we had thought.

Through the trees we were now just able to see one or two stars. Above us there was a very faint, half-ring of yellow where the sun was supposed to be. And then magically, in a twinkling, the celestial precious body burst forth and sparkled like a diamond. The ring was now complete.

'Wow,' said Quentin, 'that's cool!'

'Just a little,' I said, my mouth wide open like a goldfish. 'Just a little!'

Then rapidly the sky turned from black to grey, as the returning sun dazzled brighter. Birds who had gone to bed began singing once again. And after a while, the sky was a deep blue colour once again, and the sun, once more, a brilliant yellow ball above. We climbed down the rocks shaking and laughing and crying all at once. We had witnessed a solar eclipse! We had heard it was going to take place on the news, but had forgotten all about it since the hurricane.

The ancient Chinese used to believe that an eclipse was caused by a hungry dragon eating the sun. They used to make loud noises to scare it off. I hadn't been fooled though. I hadn't been scared, honestly! All of us knew what an eclipse was. We had learned about them the term before. When the moon moves in front of the sun, it blocks the sun's rays. This forms a shadow over the Earth. What's incredible is that we get a full eclipse here on Earth only because the sun, which is four hundred times further away than the moon is, just happens to be four hundred times bigger than the moon! Miss Dawson, I remember, had kept telling us that we mustn't look directly at the sun, as it would damage our eyes. I knew it had been an eclipse all along...I had just been pretending to be petrified!

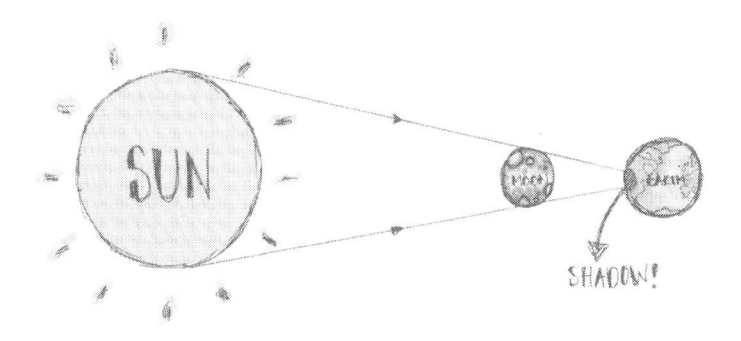

'Come on, let's get out of here,' urged Anna. We all agreed, and still shaking, began to head back to 'our beach'. We had already had way too much excitement for one day.

7 HUMAN SCALES

The next morning we awoke early. We couldn't stop thinking about the cave and the mysterious arrow carved in the rock. We had our meeting over breakfast and it was decided then that we should try to recover the rope that had been attached to our boat which had sunk. Luke, Quentin and I swam out to where the boat had gone down. The water within the reef was calm and swimming was easy. We found the boat without too much difficulty. Luckily it lay in fairly shallow water. In just a few dives we were able to untie the heavy rope from its prow and shortly afterwards the three of us were swimming back to shore - operation completed.

We were soon making our way to the lagoon and to the mysterious cave that we'd found the previous day. We hardly said a word as we followed the winding river inland. This was in stark contrast to the day before! As we scaled the edge of the waterfall, we looked down at the lagoon below. Today it looked even more perfect. Monkeys who we had spotted earlier played in the fruit trees that encircled it, and birds and butterflies of all colours danced their tropical jigs.

We crept nervously around the watery entrance once again and into the cave. Following the glow like we had done the day before, we soon reached the deeper chambers and the holes in the cave floor. Bending over them, we could see the wriggling eels way below. Each was capable of giving out eight hundred volts of electricity...OUCH!! Together they formed a river that looked like squirming brown spaghetti.

Quentin was the first to volunteer his services and none of us argued. He was strong and had always been good at climbing ropes in gym. So we fastened one end of the rope around his waist. Luke, Anna, Aisha and myself took a firm hold of the other end. As Quentin slowly edged backwards down the smaller of the two holes, we took up the strain. Then carefully, we lowered our friend down into the cavern below and towards the 'electric river'. What was the meaning of the arrow on the wall? What would he find? Or what or who would find him? Inch by inch we let the rope through our fingers and very slowly our brave friend lowered himself into the cave below.

Suddenly Quentin lurched downwards and hurtled rapidly straight towards the eels and an inevitable shocking end! The rope slid violently through our hands and the friction burned sharply as its rough surface raced cruelly across our soft skin. We were on the point of dropping the rope when Luke, in a flash, tied our end of the rope around his waist. Then without hesitating, he threw himself down through the second of the two holes. At that very moment Aisha, Anna and I were forced to let go of the rope completely. Two screams pierced the silence of the cave and echoed eerily back and forth. Then everything was still and quiet again, apart from a faint groaning that came from the chamber below.

Anxiously the three of us who were left, peered down into the first hole. There was Quentin hanging about three metres below. We then peered down into the second hole. There was the quick thinking Luke - again about three metres below. Both were hovering helplessly, only a few feet from the electric river. Luke was in quite a lot of pain where the rope had pulled tightly around his waist. If it hadn't been a matter of life and death it would have been very funny. Below us Luke and Quentin were facing each other, swinging gently back and forth. Without thinking of his own safety, Luke had saved Quentin's life. He had gambled on them being both about the same weight. So he had guessed that the force down caused by his body, would balance the force down caused by Quentin's body. It was a bit like a pair of old fashioned kitchen scales. Luckily for them both, he had been right.

'Would you stop hanging around down there,' I yelled down jokingly.

'What can you see down there?' shouted Anna. 'Are there any signs of life?'

'Nothing,' replied Quentin, 'There's a pool of eels and loads of rocks and that's it.'

'Hey hang on Quents, what's that behind you on that ledge over there?' asked Luke, squinting to try and make out what it was. Quentin spun delicately around on his rope so that he could see what Luke was pointing at.

'It's a box of some sort,' he called back, and tried to reach it. However it was just beyond his grasp. So he began to swing himself gently backwards and forwards. On his third swing he stretched out and just managed to grab the metal box from its ledge. But as soon as the box was in his hand, he began to move downward once more towards the electric river. At the same time Luke also began moving faster and faster upwards - towards the hole above him! This time it was Anna who acted quickly and calmly. In a flash she picked up a small rock and dropped it downward towards Luke.

'Catch!' she yelled. He did. But only just in time. As he caught hold of the rock, the forces on both sides of the human scales balanced once again. This helped and the boys stopped gaining speed. However, they continued to move steadily in opposite directions - one up, one down. It was definitely time for a break! I stamped down hard on the rope in front of me and the boys finally came to a halt.

'Ouchhhh,' groaned Quentin in agony, as he dangled, still clutching the metal box, only centimetres from the writhing waters below.

The 'spaghetti river' squirmed silently beneath his scrambling feet. Looking up at us, his eyes were wide with fear. He was breathing heavily and droplets of sweat were forming on his brow. We watched helplessly from above as the droplets ran together into a large bead of sweat. It ran down his cheek, stopped briefly at his chin, and then tumbled down into the waters below.

Several moments went by as the two boys fought to get their breath back. Then slowly but steadily, the two courageous cave swingers began to haul themselves up their ropes - one with stone, one with box, each tucked under an arm. As Luke's head appeared through his hole, I helped him out. At the same time the others hauled up a very dazed Quentin from *his* hole. They both slumped exhausted in front of us on the cave floor. We clapped and cheered the two of them as they lay there panting.

We left the cave immediately and climbed down to the comfort of ground level. Quentin had earned the right to open the box and when at last he had recovered properly from his ordeal, he carefully began to prize open the lid. The rest of us huddled eagerly around. We each strained to catch the first glimpse of the contents of the box. The lid came off slowly to reveal a strip of thin bark with elegant writing on it. Quentin reached into the box and pulled it out. The writing was in English, however, some of the letters were difficult to make out. Some kind of red dye had been used to write with. Slowly, Quentin began to read it out aloud.

**'The key to the mysteries
Of the whole universe
May be found by
Yourself if you sort out this verse
Because this verse leads you
On a 1,2,3,4
And then one day you'll find
The right key to the door.'**

> THE KEY TO THE MYSTERIES
> OF THE WHOLE UNIVERSE
> MAY BE FOUND BY
> YOURSELF IF YOU SORT OUT THIS VERSE
> BECAUSE THIS VERSE LEADS YOU
> ON A 1, 2, 3, 4
> AND THEN ONE DAY YOU'LL FIND
> THE RIGHT KEY TO THE DOOR.

'Excellent, I love riddles,' I said, as my brain began to search its meaning. My eyes flicked across the lines of the riddle, searching desperately for its hidden meaning.

'The key to the mysteries.
Of the whole universe…'

'To my boat! To my boat,' I blurted out within seconds. This was easy. This was an acrostic. Reading down, the initial letters of the poem spelled out 'To my boat'. What that meant though was a different matter. The line about a '1, 2, 3, 4' also hinted that this might not be the only clue.

'I guess we've got to go to their boat, wherever that is,' suggested Anna.

'The 'key to the mysteries of the whole universe', that sounds good,' said Aisha smiling. 'But who wrote this and where are they now?' These questions and dozens more, rolled around our minds as we trooped back puzzled to 'our beach' and a coconut, banana and mango lunch.

The following day we awoke extra early. We set off

promptly so that we could explore more of the island. Would we find the boat and the key to the mysteries of the universe, whatever that was? Maybe we could use the boat to sail off the island?

Anna suggested that she and Aisha should walk up the beach in an anti-clockwise direction around the island. Luke, Quentin and myself she said, should head the way we had previously gone, in a clockwise direction. The idea was that we would meet up about half way around the island. We would then cut back across the middle of the island together, over the mountainous ridge which we had climbed on the first day.

8 THAT SINKING FEELING

We three boys set off at a brisk pace. The sun was hot, but by now we were becoming used to the heat. 'I guess it's about 37°C,' said Quentin with authority.

'I guess,' I said, not really knowing. Quentin was good with numbers and was rarely wrong. I often wished I had his 'supersonic thinking' in maths, but it didn't come easily to me.

'We all have different talents,' my dad would say. I used to think he just said that to make me feel better, but I can see now that he was right. We all have something that we are good at, we just have to find out what that 'something' is.

We felt so free as we paced along the white sands. The water inside the reef was even calmer than when we'd first waded through it. It sparkled magnificently under the low sun. A thousand golden candles bobbed up and down on its surface. It was indeed tempting to go and bathe and to explore the reef and its magical secrets, but that would have to wait until another day. For now, our task was to find the boat in the riddle. We hadn't seen any boat from the high point that we had climbed on the day we had arrived. You would expect Luke to have spotted it, so perhaps it had gone - floated away. As we walked along, I continued my sketch of the island. It was crudely drawn but it would do the job.

As we rounded the bottom of the island, the land began to climb and before long we found ourselves walking along the grassy edge of a vertical cliff. We marched on without a break. Then slowly we descended to sea level once more as we approached the northern end of the island. Here the sand was a dark, greyish colour. In fact, much of the coastline was almost black!

'Over there,' cried Luke, 'I see it!' and he started running. So Quents and I ran too. We soon saw what Luke had seen, about a hundred metres from the water's edge. It was the mast of a very small wooden sailboat, sticking up at quite an angle. We could now see that the small boat was stuck fast in the ground. On one of its sides, mud came close to its edge. Luke stopped about ten metres from the boat itself and as we reached him we understood why. The ground we had run over had become extremely marshy and we were now unable to get any closer.

The boat we discovered, was surrounded by thick, gloopy, mud-like sand. I took a cautious step, transferring my weight slowly forward. But in an instant my foot had disappeared into the mud. I grabbed hold of Luke's shoulder and pulled my foot back carefully. SLURP! SLURP! It made the most brilliant rude noise ever! It was just like... Well anyway, this *must* be the boat in the riddle. But how could we get to it? It seemed impossible.

'Nothing's impossible if you set your mind to it,' my mind played back an old conversation. 'Where did that come from?' I asked myself.

Just then the girls arrived. 'We've brought some things we're going need,' said Anna smiling.

'We got here ages ago and thought these things would be useful.' She threw down the rope and the tarpaulin at our feet.

'Have you already been here?' I asked in disbelief.

'Yep,' said Anna coolly, '*And* we ran back to base because we are going to need these. You see the problem,' she explained without pausing, 'is that gravity pulls down and makes us too heavy for the sand. That's why you just sank when you stood on it. However, if we spread our weight out over a wider surface, we won't sink… or not so fast at any rate, as the pressure on the sand is less.' She then set about making a small hole in the canvas tarpaulin. She slid the rope through it and tied the rope around it with a knot. Next she walked around to the other side of the boat. She folded up the canvas into a tight ball and fastened it by tying the loose corners together. Then holding on tightly to the other end of the rope, she hurled the canvas package high over the boat towards us. It landed just in front of us and we all clapped wildly. I saw what she wanted to do.

'I'll do it,' I offered quietly, 'I'm probably the lightest.'

'You sure?' asked Luke. I said nothing but unfolded the canvas package that lay at our feet. Then sheepishly I lay down on my back on top of it, as flat I could make myself. The others joined Anna on the other side of the boat and then together they began to pull me towards the boat. I was terrified.

The mud soon began to lick over the edges of my 'mud-mobile' and my backside began to gradually sink. Slowly, very carefully, I stretched myself out as flat as I could, so my weight was spread over as big an area as possible. I closed my eyes as mud started to ooze around my ears. 'What a way to go,' I thought. 'What a horrible way to go.'

And then THUMP! My head hit the side of the boat. Swiftly, I slung my arm over the side and dragged myself up and over into the boat and lay breathless on the wooden floor. Immediately there was a creaking sound. I didn't have long. With my extra weight, the boat was now slipping deeper into its muddy grave, with me in it! Beside my foot was a green bottle, but apart from that, the boat was empty. Mud was now slopping in torrents over the sides of the boat. I was being swallowed up!

'Hurry, hurry,' yelled Quentin. I grabbed the bottle and tumbled back over the edge of the boat and on to my 'mud-mobile'. I closed my eyes and took a large gasp of breath just as the deck of the boat was sucked under the mud next to me and disappeared from view.

The others pulled me fast and it had to be. When I finally reached them and firmer ground, I was already a mud roll. They led me staggering to the water's edge and I collapsed.

When I opened my eyes, I was clean again and lying further up the beach on solid ground. The others were eating some fruit and I joined them without speaking. They smiled at me and Anna passed me the green bottle. 'Your go,' she whispered smiling.

I yanked at the cork which was half sticking out and shook the bottle. Out slid a roll of dried 'leaf paper'. I unrolled it carefully and just as we had hoped, there was another message. This time it was in two parts.

'Dear friends,' I read.

'Congratulations on finding my boat. I thought I'd leave you another couple of riddles to keep you busy.'

> CONGRATULATIONS ON FINDING MY BOAT. I THOUGHT I'D LEAVE YOU ANOTHER COUPLE OF RIDDLES TO KEEP YOU BUSY.

'Here we go again,' said Luke. I continued to read.

'It may not be the biggest one
There's bigger ones it's true
But this one's dangerous for sure
Watch out, it's time is due.

Then watch out for the animals
They'll know when it is time
So keep your senses tuned my friends
For they're your warning sign.

Make sure you have an escape plan
If you want to get home
If not, he might well catch you up
And turn you into stone.'

> IT MAY NOT BE THE BIGGEST ONE
> THERE'S BIGGER ONES IT'S TRUE
> BUT THIS ONE'S DANGEROUS FOR SURE
> WATCH OUT, ITS TIME IS DUE.
>
> THEN WATCH OUT FOR THE ANIMALS
> THEY'LL KNOW WHEN IT IS TIME
> SO KEEP YOUR SENSES TUNED MY FRIENDS
> FOR THEY'RE YOUR WARNING SIGN.
>
> MAKE SURE YOU HAVE AN ESCAPE PLAN
> IF YOU WANT TO GET HOME
> IF NOT, HE MIGHT WELL CATCH YOU UP
> AND TURN YOU INTO STONE!

'Well what do you make of that?' I said, looking around blankly at the others.

'I have no idea,' replied Luke.

'Nor me,' said Quentin.

'I don't know,' said Aisha shaking her head, 'but it doesn't sound great, does it!'

'I think I know,' said Anna quietly. 'I might not be right so…look, first I was thinking of an animal…but they normally eat you, they don't turn you into stone. So, I reckon it's something far bigger than an animal. I think may be that it's a volcano.' I read the riddle a second time.

'Yes,' said Luke as I finished reading. 'Anna, I agree. I think you're probably right. It's talking about a volcano!'

'Well,' I said, 'I can't see any volcano. It sounds like a load of rubbish to me.'

'Read the second riddle out,' said Quentin impatiently.

'Okay,' I said, and I began to read again.

**'Take the 'Y' out of yeast
And my friend you will find
The key to a feast
That to you will be kind.'**

> TAKE THE 'Y' OUT OF YEAST
> AND MY FRIEND YOU WILL FIND
> THE KEY TO A FEAST
> THAT TO YOU WILL BE KIND.

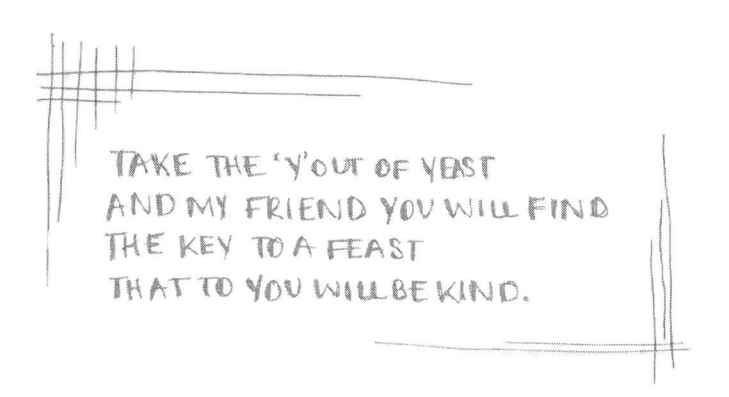

'Easy, that's too easy, that one,' said Aisha after just a few seconds. 'If you take the Y out of yeast, what do you get? You get east. The sun rises in the east, and that's over there,' she said, nodding vaguely in the direction of our landing site. 'That's how I used to remember that the sun rose in the east, because y**east** makes bread *rise*.

As we set off back to camp, Luke jogged back up the coast towards the buried boat, its wooden mast was now the only part that was visible. He came back moments later with a large ball of creamy mud. We looked at him puzzled. 'You'll see,' he grinned.

Instead of returning over the centre of the island, we decided to head back down along the beach on the eastern coast. If we were lucky, we might even find the 'key to a feast' that was written about in the riddle. It was a long walk and we didn't find the 'key' and when we arrived back at camp, we were exhausted.

'Eureka,' said Luke triumphantly. 'Eureka! Eureka!'

'What do you mean?' I said.

'Eureka, means 'I've got it'.

'I know that, but what have you got?'

He then presented us with a pint-sized model of an alien being that he'd made with the ball of mud. It had a long neck and one enormous eye that was its head. Its body was roughly triangular shaped, it had two arms and it was supported by two huge toe-less feet.

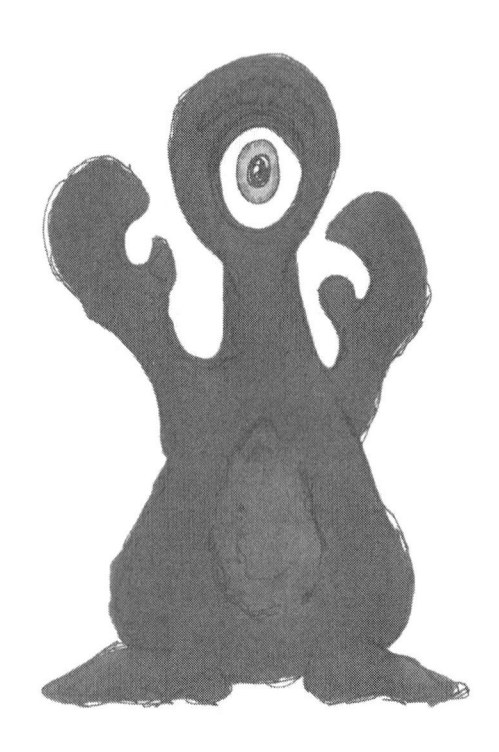

'What do you think of that?' he asked with a smirk. 'Boggo, the one-eyed clay monster! Tomorrow I'm going to leave him in the sun and he should harden up. He's going to be our mascot.'

9 CARNIVOROUS CRAVINGS

Saturday arrived, but there was no weekend T.V. or computer gaming for us. Instead, swimming, diving and exploring beckoned. Oh, and of course clay modelling! Luke placed Boggo in the sun and he and the others went for a swim in the bay. I chose to go hunting for food. My stomach often makes decisions for me and well, a stomach can't be wrong, can it?

So off I went, stomach first and the rest of me not far behind. I was really fed up with bananas, mangoes and coconuts. Nice as they were, they were becoming a trifle tiresome. I craved something different, something meaty, something chewy. As images of burgers and steaks flashed across my mind, I was determined to satisfy my carnivorous cravings!

I hadn't gone far when I heard a noise that froze me to the spot. There was something in front of me. It came from behind some bushes and I didn't like the sound of it one bit. Nervously I crouched down and peered through the leaves. Then a smile crept over my face and all the way down to my belly. On the other side of the bush was a walking 'butcher's shop'. No less than six pig-like creatures were munching away amongst the bushes, with satisfied grunts. In a flash I sneaked back to the gang and shared my news. The idea of a Sunday roast impressed them. Together we planned how we would, err…how we would, err… kill the pig. Soon we arrived at the following plan:

PLAN
1. **Dig a large hole**
2. **Cover the hole with sticks and camouflage it with leaves**
3. **Chase the pigs in the direction of the pit**
4. **Serve with roast potatoes and gravy**

Digging was really hard work using sticks and stones. However soon, with the five of us mucking in, we were satisfied that the pig pit was deep enough. We placed thin sticks over it and then covered these over with leaves. It was good. It was really good. It was *so* good that we had to be careful not to fall into the pit ourselves. 'Now for our sheepdog act,' I announced with a bark. We made our way quietly behind the pigs and in all that time they had only wandered a few metres away. We spread ourselves out into an arc. Then, on my signal, we began to charge towards our pink targets, yelling at the top of our voices.

With squeals of surprise and terror, the pigs fled in the direction of our trap. For several moments all was frantic. The noise was thunderous. Bushes shook violently. There were squeals and grunts and yelping and shouting. From a distance, you couldn't make out who was chasing who! And then all of a sudden, everything went very, very still and quiet. The pigs had all vanished, all that is, except one. It lay motionless, at the bottom of our pit. Our plan had worked. We could hardly believe it! We had caught our first pig (and it had died on impact, which was definitely a good thing).

Quentin was the first to jump down into the pit to haul out the pig. Luke and I soon joined him. But it was only then that we realised that our plan had one *big* weakness. As we tried to move our prize, it dawned on us that we were never going to be able to lift it up out of the hole. It was a fairly small pig, as pigs go, but it had a large mass and so it was very, very heavy. We pulled it. We yanked it. We shouted at it. But it was not going to budge. We all sat around the pit, and stared glumly down at our Sunday roast, covered in hair and dust. I can speak for all us I think, we all felt a bit silly. I felt the worst as it had been my plan.

'Whoops,' I said. 'Anna, I think you should have planned ahead better.'

'*Who* should have planned better ahead?' she said grumpily. 'Nah, I'm just pulling your leg!' she continued, with a kind smile. 'It's not your fault. None of us thought it through properly.'

'You've got it,' said Quentin, turning to Anna.

'Got what?' Anna replied.

'We've got to pull its leg. It's the only way. We've got to *drag* it out. Pass me that notepad.' I passed Quentin the notepad and he started to scribble frantically.

'If we dig a slope here on the edge of the pit,' he explained, pointing to his sketch. 'If we cut the side away like this, it will be like a ramp and we can then drag 'Piggy' up it, like how they pull boats out of the sea and on to land.'

So we dug and dug and dug a most wonderful slope and it only took us about four hours! However, we were exhausted by the time we'd finished the ramp and when we tried to pull Piggy up it, he barely moved. It did budge a little, but we still could not pull it up the rough gravely slope.

'What a pig,' I said, 'The ground is just too rough, there's too much friction, we'll never do it. I'm sorry, it's all my fault. It's all been a waste of time.' Again we slumped exhausted around the edge of the pit, utterly dejected.

'What do you mean 'too much friction?'' asked Quentin puzzled.

'You remember,' I said. 'To move something, you need a force right?'

'Yeah.'

'Well, we're all pulling with a force, but that big hairy pig is rubbing on the ground and stopping us pulling it out. That's the friction. That's a force too.'

'Okay Einstein,' said Aisha, 'What can we do about it? Can we make the friction less?' I looked blankly at the others and shrugged my shoulders.

It was then that Luke came up with an idea. Once again it was the canvas tarpaulin from the boat that came to our rescue. Luke ran off quickly to fetch it from the camp and when he returned with it a short while later, part three of our operation commenced. We shoved it under the pink hairy mass and tied the corners of the tarpaulin together, so the pig was wrapped up, apart from its front two legs that were sticking out. 'There,' said Luke, glowing with pride, 'less friction.'

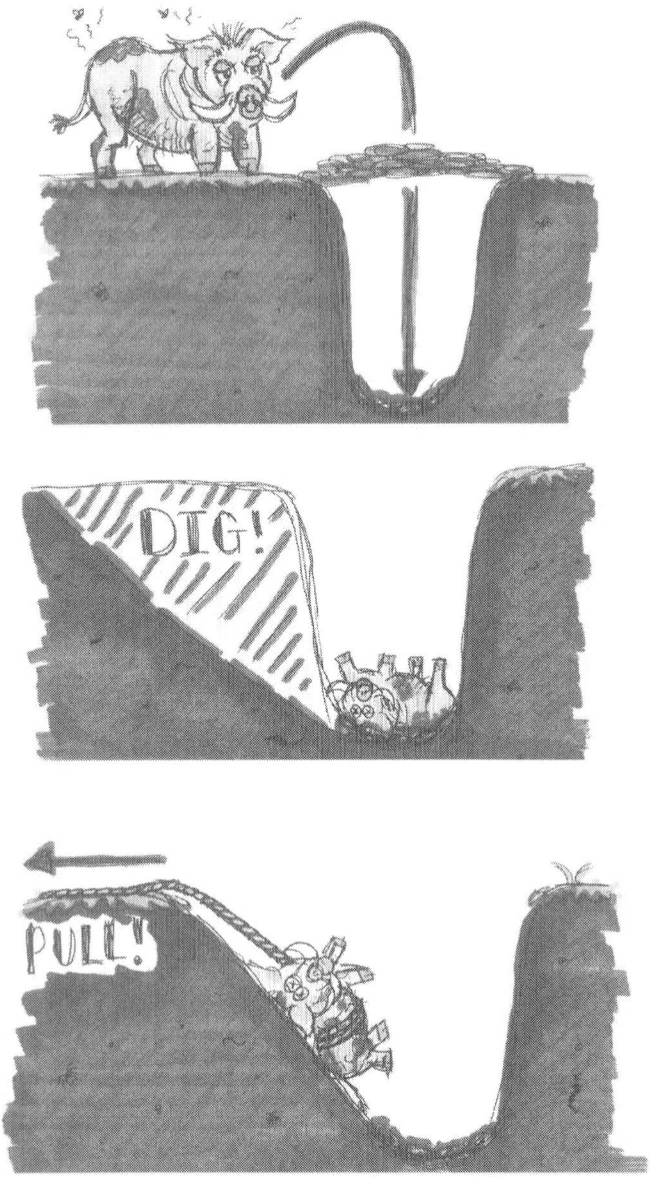
DIG!
PULL!

He was right too. Between us we were then able to pull the hairy pink mass, on the tarpaulin, up the ramp. It was a 'smooth operation!' What's more, with the pig on its 'friction reducer', we began to drag it without too much trouble, across the forest floor. It did get tiring, but with four of us pulling, one resting and using a rotation system, we forced our way on. The thought of our tasty reward the next day kept us all going. As we weaved in and out of the trees and bushes, we began to make up a song all about forces. And by the time we eventually staggered into camp in full song, we had mastered a full four verses.

'We are the forces
We push and pull and twist
We make things move and we make things stop
We slow things down and
We speed em up.
(Bm didi bm didi bm bm bm)

Now gravity is a special force
It pulls things down to the ground
If we didn't have gravity
While sitting on the lavatory
We'd all start floating around.
(Bm didi bm didi bm bm bm)

Friction too is a force you know
That can really rub you up the wrong way
It can cause an awful snag
As it can be a mighty drag
And lead to quite a delay.
(Bm didi bm didi bm bm bm)

**Now if you want something to move left
You must push it more from the right
And if you're pushing from the front
While someone's pushing from the back
You might well be there all night.
(Bm didi bm didi bm bm bm)'**

We made up the 'Bm didi bm' bit later, which is sung, but this is optional. And by the way, 'lavatory' is an old fashioned name for the toilet!

On arrival we were greeted by Boggo, who was waiting patiently for us, where Luke had left him.

10 FACT OR FRICTION?

That night we all slept soundly and dreamed of roast pork, roast potatoes, crackling, fresh mint peas and gravy. When we awoke, we set to work at once to prepare our feast. We boys were far too squeamish to cut the pig up into smaller pieces, so we left that to the two girls who did a great job. They used some sharp stones that we had found to rip through the tough skin of the animal and to gouge out hunks of pig flesh. Meanwhile, Luke and I set about making a fire, while Quentin was left to gather together some vegetables.

Making a fire is not as easy as it looks in books or in films when you don't happen to have a handy box of matches. What's more, the sun wasn't hot enough yet to use the old 'glasses' method, as Luke found out.

'So what are we going to do then?' complained Luke, after stubbornly trying with his glasses for over twenty minutes without success.

'Well, I once read that you can rub two sticks together to make a spark. Do that near some tinder that will catch alight and voila!'

'What's tinder?' asked Luke. I explained that tinder was dry material like small pieces of dried stick or grasses that catch alight easily. He agreed that it was worth giving it a go. So, we both rummaged around and fairly soon found some suitable pieces of wood, one sharp stick to use as a 'drill' and a flatter piece of wood for a base. Onto the base we placed some bits of tinder that we had also gathered. Then, rolling the stick quickly between the palms of our hands, we drilled as fast as we could into the base with the pointed end. The faster we rubbed the sticks together, the more friction it created. The more friction it created, the hotter it got. Again and again we tried - but nothing. Our hands were now getting raw – just like the pig meat!

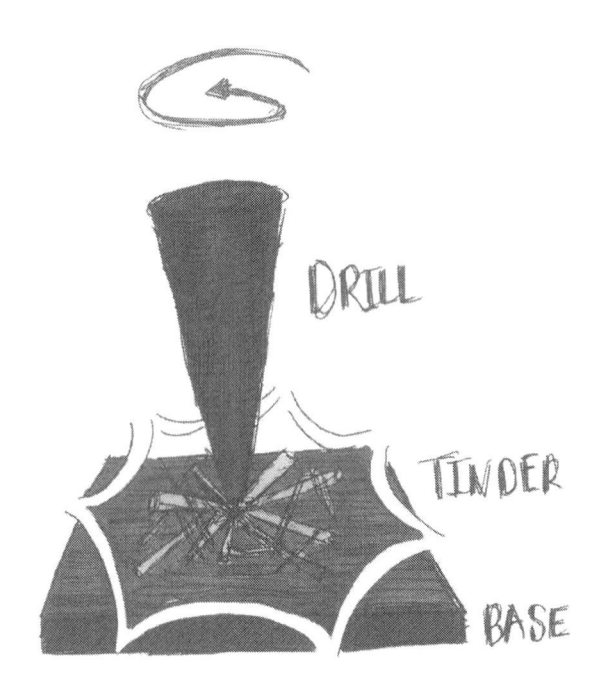

'Oh great,' sighed Luke impatiently, 'raw pig, just what I fancy, don't you?' We tried again, and again and then again. And then we tried one more time for luck. Then we tried another time for luck. And then after that, we tried once more. And then the last time we tried, cheered on by our extremely desperate stomachs, and to mighty applause from the others, it happened. Just when we were about to give up, it happened! Fire! We actually had fire! Okay, so it was the smallest, tiniest fire you have ever seen, *but* fires, like the bellies of grown-ups, grow rapidly if they are left to do their own thing. And it was not too long therefore, before we could smell our delicious pork steaks sizzling away merrily in our super mini ovens that we had made from two of the empty Coke cans that we still had.

Instead of potatoes, we had roast bananas. And instead of vegetables, we had roast bananas. We cooked them in their skins. They were delicious! As you know, I am extremely fussy about my food. Well, I felt that it really needed just a small sprinkle of salt - just to bring out the flavour. So off I ran, down to one of the rockpools and scraped together a few crystals of sea-salt that had been left behind when the water had evaporated off. That was the finishing touch. The meal was incredible! Fresh pork steaks, roast bananas - amazing!

That afternoon we just relaxed. We lazed around by the camp and swam in the warm waters of the lagoon. Luke found some blackberries and he used the juice to paint Boggo a funny purple colour. I however, couldn't wait until Monday so that we could get on with looking for the next clue.

The calendar tree showed eight marks. I was already feeling pretty homesick. I think we all were. I also kept thinking about the volcano. Did it really exist? Or was the riddle pointing to something else? If it was a volcano, where was it? And was it still active? There was no obvious evidence that it had erupted in the recent past. If it did erupt, we had nowhere to escape to. We would be doomed like those people in Pompei, in Italy.

In our Monday morning meeting we decided to split up and look for the clue on the east side of the island. We arranged to meet up back at the camp when the sun was directly overhead. So off we set, each one of us determined to find the 'key to the feast'.

When the sun had swung to its highest point, we stopped searching and each headed back to camp as planned. Luke was last of course, but he wasn't too late.

'Anybody found it?' I asked hopeful. Nobody had found anything. We rested for a while before resuming our search. Again…nothing. Evening came and we sat around another fire and tucked into some more pork chops. We watched the sun set over the water. Slowly it dropped in the sky, growing larger as it fell. By the time it reached the sea, it had become a huge golden orb. For a moment it seemed we could walk right over to it, across the sea, which now sparkled and formed a carpet of gold, leading to a faraway treasure.

And what a treasure it was. Our sun, a star, one of billions; but to us, special. Our sun, that gives energy and life to our little planet. 'Eight minutes is what it takes,' I remembered my Dad saying. 'Eight minutes for its light to reach us.' Just as the waves were coming towards us now and breaking on the reef, the sun's light was coming towards us in waves, but much, much faster! About one hundred and fifty million kilometres in eight minutes. That's pretty fast isn't it! If you tried to drive to the sun in a car, Dad had told me once, it would take you over a hundred and fifty years!

One moment the sun was sitting on the water, the next, it had slipped below the horizon. It left a criss-cross of purples, yellows and reds that was different from every other sunset there had ever been. No one had ever seen *this* sunset. And tomorrow's would be different again - perhaps with a whisper of cloud, or with a family of pelicans heading south?

The magic was broken in a split second. Luke was already running down to the water's edge, waving his arms frantically. 'Plane! Plane!' he yelled. We joined him in a flash. Then we saw it. A small dot in the sky, but it was coming our way. We were saved! We were going home! We would soon be seeing our families and friends. This was it! Aisha had been right. They had been looking for us. And now they had found us.

'Over here. Here we are.' We screamed, waving and shouting frantically and jumping up and down excitedly. The small dot came closer and closer, but it was so high, so high. It passed the entire length of the island and then continued on without changing its course.

'It was never going to see us,' I groaned, as tears swelled up in my eyes. 'It was too far away. It was too high. And the light's not good enough. It *didn't* see us.' The plane disappeared from view and we trudged glumly back up the beach.

'Come on you guys, heads up, positive,' said Aisha, still determined as ever. 'It might be back tomorrow at the same time, and then we'll be ready for it. We'll light a huge fire here on the beach. They're bound to spot us then.'

And so, the following day we scavenged for sticks and dried grasses that we would be able to light quickly. By afternoon we had built a decent sized bonfire and early that evening, we lit a small fire next to it as a 'pilot light' from which we would light our signal.

We waited for the plane to return, poised to light our bonfire, our signal to the world that we were here, that we were alive! But that evening we didn't see the plane. It didn't return the next evening either, nor the next, nor the one after that. And the days rolled on. We watched the sun rise and the sun set. We watched the moon rise and the moon set. We watched as the moon changed from a thin 'C' to a big bright 'O', and then to a thin backwards 'C'. And that was a month! And we watched many 'C's' and many 'O's come and go.

And we never found the 'key to the feast', although we searched hard for it. Gradually we stopped looking and spent our time on other projects. We made ourselves busy by making tools from stones and making clay pots for cooking and carrying water.

We came to know our end of the island fairly well and it was truly beautiful. It was a wash of golds, greens and blues. There were a thousand surprises wherever you went. Brooks bubbled on their way to the sea and watered lush vegetation dripping with a huge variety of fruits. Butterflies, dragonflies, birds and insects skipped across beams of yellow that leapt from the canopy above. It was a circus of colour, of light, of magical sounds and of sweet perfumes and it was our home! But it wasn't really home. In fact, home was something that we never spoke about. And we tried not to think about it.

We often went swimming around the coral reef. It was amazing. It was just like a rainforest - but underwater. It was the home of more fish than you could count. And it was the habitat of many other animals too: sea-urchins, jellyfish, starfish, squid, octopus...

Once when I was swimming out by the reef, I turned a corner and there it was. Two huge eyes looking at me! It was of course an alien sent on a mission to seek me out and destroy me. Well, that was my initial reaction. 'Alien attack,' I screamed. But it came out as 'Blabplibplm blabplab'. I swallowed a mouthful of salty water which almost choked me. However, it did bring me back to my senses. What I was actually staring at, was a cute looking baby octopus, no more than eight inches wide. I later nicknamed him 'Goggles'.

We loved exploring the reef. Its branches twisted and turned upwards towards the light. Some were like Christmas trees, sharp and pointed. Others were flat like large hands catching sunshine.

Luke knew quite a lot about coral. He told me once that the branches are built by tiny sea creatures. These creatures he said, turn seawater into that white, crunchy stuff that you find at the bottom of a kettle. Limestone I think he called it. He said that the creatures cover themselves in this limestone and then they die one on top of the other! And that's how the coral branches grow bigger and bigger. Most of the coral is dead and it's only the outside of the coral that's alive.

It was the lagoon however that was my favourite place on the island. I liked to go and swim there on my own. I especially loved going there in the early evening as the last beads of sunlight threaded through the leaves. The water was warm and soft and it felt like bathing in silk.

11 TWO BERRY ANNA

It was Saturday morning. Well, it was for us at any rate. Like most mornings, I opened my eyes and gazed up into a perfect blue sky. A brisk breeze rose off the sea and helped cool us. With it came the fresh smell of the salt sea. We had become more used to the heat on the island, although some days it still felt too hot to do much.

'Why is it blue?' I wondered.

'What?' called out Aisha who was sitting under a nearby palm tree?

'Sorry I was just thinking. The sky, why is it blue and not green or brown or some other colour?'

'Well,' she said, 'Remember I explained that the sun's light is made up from all the colours of the rainbow? Well, you know the air is made up of tiny, tiny particles that we can't see. When the sun's rays hit these particles, the rays bounce back and are '*bent*' in new directions. More blue light bounces back in our direction, towards us down here on Earth, than any of the other colours. That's why the sky looks blue to us.'

'Ah, thanks,' I said sleepily.

'So why does the sky look red in the evening?' my brain asked me. 'Quiet brain,' I retorted. 'It's too early, go back to sleep.' I tried to doze off again but I couldn't. Aisha was singing something under her breath. I think it went like this:

**'Bendy Blue,
Bendy Blue,
Bends much more
Into our view.
That is why,
It is true,
The sky above
Seems blue
To YOU!'**

That morning, Anna had gone off early on one of her strolls, which she liked to take to clear her mind. The rest of us were lazier. We lay around under the trees, still half-snoozing, half soaking in the morning sun. I missed my bed back home, but there is something amazing about a sandy bed and feeling the sun's orange warmth seep into your body.

'If the sun is so far away,' I thought, 'it must be a really hot...'

'Fifteen million degrees centigrade,' said Quentin.

'Oh sorry Quents, I thought I was only talking to myself.'

'No, you're talking out loud again. We've been listening to your conversation for the last ten minutes.'

'Sorry.' I said, a little embarrassed. What else had I said?

Just then I became aware of a figure slowly moving towards us along the beach. 'It must be Anna,' I thought, but she seemed to be bent forward and walking very sluggishly.

'Is that Anna?' I called out to the others, 'What's she doing?'

Then all of a sudden the figure slumped forward and fell to the ground. We were up and running in an instant. And as we drew closer we could see that it was indeed Anna.

'Anna, what's up?' called Luke as we reached her. She didn't reply. She was face down and her dark hair was spread over the white sand. 'What's wrong?' We rolled her over onto her back. Her face was white and her eyes were barely open. Her skin felt cold, yet her forehead was wet with sweat.

'Anna, what's happened?' pleaded Aisha, with tears in her eyes. 'What's wrong with you?' She raised Anna up slightly and cradled her in her arms. A faint groan came from Anna's lips, but no words. She slowly held out a limp hand towards us. Her hand opened and two small reddish berries rolled out through her fingers and onto the white sand below.

'Poison,' whispered Quentin, 'She's been poisoned!' Suddenly panic swept over us like a flood. Our friend had eaten some poisonous berries and she was dying in front of us. Our friend was going to die!

'Anna wake up, wake up!' begged Luke, slapping her face. But Anna's eyes stayed shut. She was barely conscious now and her breathing, we noticed, was very shallow. We stared at each other in icy silence. We each shared the same desperate, helpless look.

'Come on!' I yelled. 'Let's do *something*. She can't die, she just can't.'

'Quick,' said Quentin 'help me put her on her side.' We did as he said. Then, holding her head with one arm, he poked his finger into her mouth and down her throat. She jerked forward violently and coughed, then threw up over the sand. She then slumped back heavily into Quentin's arms.

After a while, Anna seemed to begin to breathe more deeply. Time passed and we sat anxiously around our friend, helping her to sip some water from a coconut shell. Colour eventually began to trickle back into her pale face, but her eyes remained closed. She then fell into a deep sleep and continued her gradual recovery as she dreamt. We watched over her, still anxious, but no longer gripped by panic.

We then carried Anna back to camp and laid her down on the warm sand. She slept all that day and all through the night without stirring. Several times during her sleep she kept muttering something about a rock. We couldn't make out what she was saying, but we didn't wake her. Her body knew best what she needed, whilst it sorted itself out and that was sleep.

Anna finally came around early the next morning and was desperate for water. When at last she finished drinking, we told her what had happened and how Quentin had saved her life. She then slowly began to remember things. After a while she stood up and wandered down across the beach, then gazed back over the island. She seemed to be searching for something.

'There,' she cried, 'look, that's what I saw yesterday.' We followed her gaze over the trees and up towards the mountains.

'I can see it,' announced Luke.

'Yeah me too,' I said. I hadn't noticed it before now. But way up above the tree line, along the rocks, there was something shining brightly in the sun. The sun was reflecting off the rocks too, but this thing that Anna had noticed was very different. It was shining and glistening much more brightly than everything around it.

'That's where I tried to go yesterday morning, when I ate those berries,' said Anna. 'I think I got near to it, but I just couldn't find it. On the way back I was hungry…What do you think it is?' We had no idea.

'Well, who's coming?' asked Quentin enthusiastically. No one else wanted to go just yet. It was another scorching day and it would be a long and difficult climb. 'Come on. Aisha, you'll come won't you? I need some company and another pair of eyes.' Aisha caved in.

'Oh all right Quentin, I'll come with you, but I'm not spending hours searching for it.'

The two of them filled up with supplies from camp and we watched them set off along the beach and then disappear between the trees.

12 QUENTIN'S QUEST

We didn't see them again until early that evening. I spotted them first as they burst out of the trees not far from where we were sitting. I'm sure I spotted Quentin's beaming grin before anything else. He and Aisha joined us by our little fire and we ate together beneath a magnificent blood-red sky.

Then Quents began to spout out their story. He couldn't keep it in any longer. Aisha didn't get in a word. She sat there patiently and listened with the rest of us.

'Well,' he kicked off. 'We know why you couldn't find the 'shining rock' Anna. We had the same problem. One minute we could see it – the next it had gone. We tried to reach it from all directions. Each time we thought we had got close to it, we lost sight of it. I almost gave up. In fact I would have done. Aisha kept me going,' he smiled, 'and I'm glad she did. You see, it only shines when the sun is in certain positions. We were standing right by it and then…then it caught the sun and we saw it. It was odd. It was a rock. It was a blackish colour, about the size of a small car (I'd forgotten them). But all over it, just stuck there, were hundreds of nails and other small bits of metal. They were just stuck there. No glue, no nothing. They were just stuck! I guessed straight away,' continued Quentin.' The rock that Anna had seen was magnetic, a giant magnet! It must have been made out of iron like the centre of the Earth. We know the Earth is a gigantic magnet right? That's why it has a magnetic North and South Pole. Anyway, then I had this idea,' he looked up to check we were still listening. We were, but Aisha was yawning. 'I could make a magnet, I thought! I remembered how. It's easy. All you do is 'stroke' a piece of metal, lots of times, on something else that is magnetic.'

Quentin then demonstrated how to 'stroke' a piece of metal on an invisible cat, (but it ran off quickly). 'And that's it - nothing to it. It doesn't work with all metals, but iron nails work. So that's what I used, some of the nails, and look,' he said proudly. He reached into his pocket and pulled out two small iron nails stuck to each other like a pair of magnets.

He seemed a little upset that we didn't clap. But I for one couldn't see how on earth two magnets could help us on a deserted island. Then Quentin's grin crept slowly back again. 'Watch,' he said. We watched. Aisha yawned again. Quentin picked up the half-a-coconut shell and filled it with seawater. He placed it in the sand in front of him and then gently rested one of his nails onto a leaf and set the leaf afloat on the water. As soon as Quentin took his fingers off the leaf, it spun around slowly to point in another direction. He did this several times until he was happy. Each time the leaf and the nail seemed to end up pointing in the same direction. 'North, that's north,' he said, puffing out his chest. 'And that ladies and gentlemen, is the 'Quentin Compass'. This time we all did clap – even Aisha. I still couldn't see how the 'Quentin Compass' was going to help in any way. We knew it was north already because of where the sun rose and set. It was still clever though and Quentin deserved his applause.

13 NUMBER 1, PALM TREES COURT

We had been sleeping under the stars near where we had first landed for many nights now. Although it was fairly comfortable, we had only the tarpaulin canvas for cover. The days rolled on. We decided during one of our morning meetings that it would be a good idea to build some form of more permanent shelter.

'I do think we need to plan for a rainy day,' said Anna. 'Besides, some nights it gets pretty cold, and if we get wet too, that won't be much fun.'

'Right,' chipped in Anna, 'if we're going to build something, let's do it properly and make a decent job of it. I suggest we each sketch a few ideas and then come up with a master plan.'

It was agreed. The tide was going out, so we wandered down towards the shore. There the moist sand was ideal for drawing in, with sticks or fingers. This was when our short careers as architects began. Naturally we each felt that our own idea was superior. And so it came down to a discussion and then a vote...then an argument, (not our first)...then another vote. This gave the same result as the first vote, but everyone seemed quite happy this time.

'We need a sloping roof so the rain runs off it,' stated Aisha, whose dad was in construction.

'Yes, and I need the entrance facing east, so we get the sun in the morning and a good sea view,' added Luke.

'Well I quite fancy a conservatory and a jacuzzi to relax in after work,' chuckled Quentin, getting rather childish. 'And where will we put the flatscreen?'

Eventually, after a fair amount of squabbling (yes, that's right squabbling) we arrived peacefully at our final draft. I jotted this down on one of the last remaining pages from my notebook.

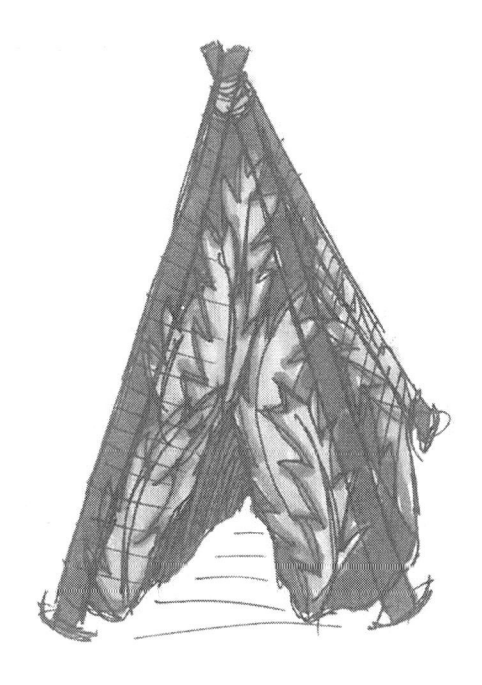

We felt comfortable staying near to where we had been sleeping up to then. For one thing, it seemed safe enough there and secondly, we would have a good view of any boats if they passed by the island. We agreed (yes that's right agreed) to move up the beach slightly and tuck ourselves just into the tree-line. Here the ground would be firmer and there was more shelter. And so it was, that after much grown up debate and precise planning, we got to work on building our dream island-home.

Aisha organised us in military fashion and assigned us each specific tasks. She and Aisha began to clear an area for our shelter, Luke and Quentin set off in search of trees and branches and I went to collect lots and lots of 'jungle string'. Well that's what we called it. It hung down from the trees further inland and was as tough as any string we had at home. We were even able to swing on the thicker strands, just like in the movies!

'Okay let's leave it there,' ordered Sergeant Major Aisha, early that evening. 'It looks like we've probably got enough materials. I suggest we leave it for now and crack on with it again at sunrise tomorrow.'

'Yes ma'am...whatever you say,' retorted Quentin, stamping out a salute.

For some reason we really felt the cold that night and this added to our motivation to have a roof over our heads. Even as dawn was breaking, we were up and scoffing down our breakfast. Next to my sketch of the shelter, I jotted down the stages that were needed to build it. If we wrote them down I thought, that would make it clearer in our heads.

'How to build a shelter
1 Choose exact site
2 Clear surface of plants and leaves. Check for roots and ants nests
3 Mark out camp dimensions on ground
4 Construct main framework

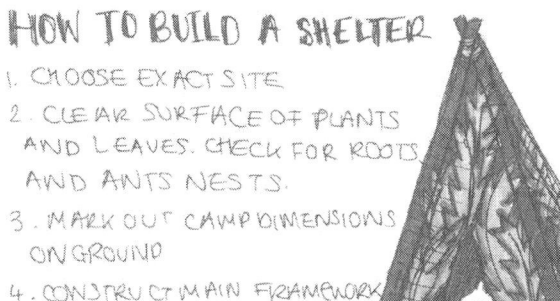

5 Dig three holes for framework to sit in
6 Sit framework poles in holes and fill with soil
7 Secure walls with branch poles. Secure into ground
8 Cover whole framework with our tarpaulin
9 Cover with leafy branches
10 Add a door of branches (use jungle string to tie them together)'

HOW TO BUILD A SHELTER

1. CHOOSE EXACT SITE
2. CLEAR SURFACE OF PLANTS AND LEAVES. CHECK FOR ROOTS AND ANTS NESTS.
3. MARK OUT CAMP DIMENSIONS ON GROUND
4. CONSTRUCT MAIN FRAMEWORK
5. DIG THREE HOLES FOR FRAMEWORK TO SIT IN.
6. SIT FRAMEWORK POLES IN HOLES AND FILL WITH SOIL.
7. SECURE WALLS WITH BRANCH POLES. SECURE INTO GROUND
8. COVER WHOLE FRAMEWORK WITH OUR TARPAULIN
9. COVER WITH LEAFY BRANCHES
10. ADD A DOOR OF BRANCHES (USE JUNGLE STRING TO TIE THEM TOGETHER)

STEP THREE

STEP FOUR

STEP TEN

Well, we all pulled together brilliantly. And that I think, was our secret – teamwork. Because by the end of that day, we were proud owners of the first luxury, detached home, on the whole of the island!

'What shall we call it?' I asked as we stood back and admired our creation. 'We must have an address.'

'How about 'Number 1, Palm Trees Court, The Island?' said Anna with a smile.

'That's good,' said Aisha, 'Number 1, Palm Trees Court it is. Going once, going twice. Sold to the lady in the corner.'

So I guess that's how we became the first official human inhabitants of the island.

Luke made a clay nameplate on which he engraved **'1, Palm Trees Court'** in flowery writing. With some jungle string, he fixed it to a nearby tree outside the entrance; just so the postman wouldn't miss us. Finally, all the way around the camp, we bashed in some short wooden stakes into the ground. I don't really know why, but it made us feel more secure somehow. We were marking out our territory like cats and other animals do with their scent.

Well it took a little getting used to; us sleeping under cover again. However, it was certainly warmer at night and during the day it gave us much needed relief from the blazing sun. Soon enough it did begin to feel like home sweet home, but it wasn't very long at all before our handiwork was put to the test.

Only a week after we had finished 'Number 1, Palm Trees Court', we were enjoying a particularly hot, humid day. The five of us were swimming inside the reef and exploring the magical secrets of the honeycomb of rock pools. Each pool was a unique garden with its own personality and charm. If you looked closely, they each had distinct miniature landscapes of valleys and mountains. Each one had taken its own hostages that had visited it at high tide and which would be held captive until the next high tide, when they could swim, or float away. There were beautiful shells, both weird and wonderfully shaped. There were small fish, anemones, starfish and other masters of disguise. Some lay invisible, waiting, watching and then darting away at our slightest movement.

Way out towards the horizon in the east, Luke suddenly noticed the dark line of a weather-front. It appeared to be heading our way. At first however, we took no notice. We hadn't seen a drop of rain since we'd been on the island. However, the dark line took no notice of our 'no notice' and marched towards us like a great army of warriors. All of a sudden the wind began to billow and the palm leaves rustled together threateningly. The warriors rolled on towards us. In the distance lightning flashes flickered and flared on their black stage, while their twins mirrored them in the waters below.

'One hundred, two hundred, three hundred,' we counted. Then came the rumble - the '*click*' of the giant spark that we had seen jump from the sky moments earlier. It was an awesome sight. Such power! 'If mankind could only capture this energy,' I thought, 'and store it like in a battery, well, there would be enough energy to light whole cities!'

The heavenly tap then abruptly opened above us. A million raindrops began pelting the beach around us forming a million dimples in the sand. In the same way meteorites had once pelted the surface of the moon to form its craters.

We made our way swiftly up the beach, protecting our

eyes from the sand that was now being whipped up by fierce gusts of wind. We bundled into our shelter already soaked, as the storm raged outside. This was all too familiar. This was how our nightmare had begun. The memory flooded my body with fear. The claps of thunder chased their flashes and soon caught up with them. The storm had moved directly above us. No time to count. Through tiny holes in the walls we watched. Wind-bent trees danced wildly to the flashing and crashing of the tropical storm and waves battered the shore.

'How do the counts between the thunder and the flash tell you how far away the storm is?' bellowed Aisha over the din.

'Well,' I yelled back, hardly able to hear my own voice, 'the boom and the flash happen at exactly the same time. The boom is actually the noise of the gigantic 'sky-spark'. Because the flash travels super-fast, you see that straight away. But the boom travels slower than the flash, so it takes longer to get to you.'

'I see,' she yelled, her eyes lighting up. 'So if the storm is really close, the lightening only just beats the boom...but if the storm is a long way off, the spark has more time to get ahead and the boom gets to you much later. Is that right?'

'You've got it!' I shouted back.

Time passed. Slowly, the thunderclaps softened into growls and the growls slowly dropped behind their flashes...three hundred, four hundred, five hundred...We each breathed a sigh of relief. 'Number 1, Palm Trees Court' had overcome its first hurdle. Over the other side of the island, where it was still raining heavily, the sun squeezed itself through the dark cloud. Like in the spray in the waterfall, the sunlight split up into its different parts. We wandered down to the water's edge and looked back over the island, where a magnificent double rainbow hung majestically above us.

14 KNOCK KNOCK

We tried to remain positive, although this was not always easy. I joked that our 'calendar tree' would soon fall over with all the marks that we were making on it! Last count was 206 days - almost three hundred thousand minutes, according to Quentin - and I'm sure we forgot to mark it some mornings.

However, we all got on well as a team, and if we did happen to fall out, we had a rule that we must make up before we went to sleep. We found this was important, as all of us made mistakes. By making up and forgiving each other before we slept, each day was a fresh start. In this way, we were able to stay best friends.

We also discovered that each of us had different skills. Luke of course was the observant one. He saw things that other people didn't. It wasn't that his eyesight was any better than ours; in fact he needed glasses. The difference however was that he observed the world around him closely.

Anna was the 'thinker'. She was good at planning things carefully and solving problems, like she did on the boat with the 'salt-separator'. She was what you would call analytical or 'Annalytical!'

Quentin, well he was a 'walking calculator'. Quentin equals maths. And then there was Aisha. She was our battery-pack. She gave us energy. Always cheery, she never gave up. She always kept trying, even if things didn't work out. And myself, well I guess I was good at writing things down and recording things.

However, an amazing thing began to happen. We all started to pick up each other's skills. For instance, Anna picked up on Luke's skill of observation. Remember it was Anna who had noticed the 'shining rock' and it was Anna, as it turned out, who eventually found the 'Key to the feast' from the last riddle that we had found. If you'd forgotten the riddle, this is how it went:

'Take the 'Y' out of yeast
And my friend you will find
The key to a feast
That to you will be kind.'

> TAKE THE 'Y' OUT OF YEAST
> AND MY FRIEND YOU WILL FIND
> THE KEY TO A FEAST
> THAT TO YOU WILL BE KIND.

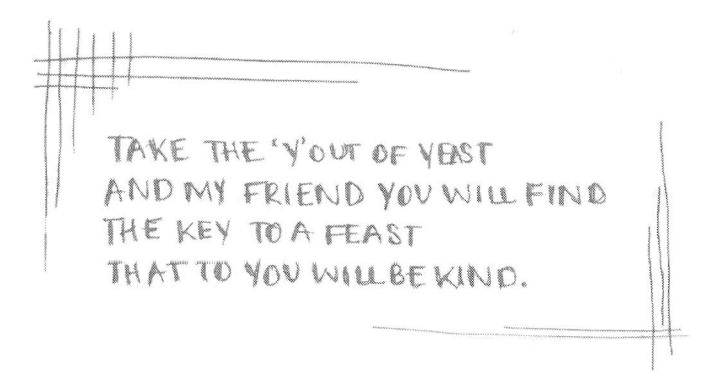

It happened one morning, many, many weeks after we'd found the riddle and after we had given up entirely on finding the 'key'. That morning Anna got up early for a morning walk, whilst the rest of us were still sleeping. We were woken up when she called to us through the entrance of the shelter. A broad grin was splashed right across her face. 'Come, follow me,' she said. She then led us up the beach no more than three hundred yards and pointed towards the treeline.

'What?' said Quentin.

'Look just in there, about two metres in.'

Only as we approached the trees, could I see it however. It was a palm tree, one of thousands on the island. On this tree however, someone had carved the shape of a door into its trunk.

'Where do people put keys?' Anna asked smiling. She then stepped forward to the tree and reached down to where the keyhole was carved. Slowly she put her fingers into the small key hole in the tree trunk. Then carefully she drew out a tiny green bottle with a small cork in it. She pulled out the cork and shook out a smaller, but now familiar piece of rolled up leaf-paper inside.

Like Luke, Anna had learnt how to really look; how to observe. We had walked over that part of the beach many, many times, but had never really noticed the tree. That is so often the case isn't it! We see things, but don't really see them. We look at people, but don't really see people. We listen to people, but don't really hear them. Anna had looked properly and she had found what she was looking for. She turned to us with a big smile, before starting to read.

> 'Well done my friends, you're getting hot
> I knew you'd find the tree
> So now let's take another step
> With riddle number three.

To solve this clue in one lifetime
I must reflect along the line
That travels from the south to north
And there you'll find the precious fourth.

To aid you on this little quest
I have a splendid view of west
I hide away deep in the past
Where the rising tide will reach me last.'

> WELL DONE MY FRIENDS, YOU'RE GETTING HOT
> I KNEW YOU'D FIND THE TREE
> SO NOW LET'S TAKE ANOTHER STEP
> WITH RIDDLE NUMBER THREE.
>
> TO SOLVE THIS CLUE IN ONE LIFETIME
> I MUST REFLECT ALONG THE LINE
> THAT TRAVELS FROM THE SOUTH TO NORTH
> AND THERE, YOU'LL FIND THE PRECIOUS FOURTH.
>
> TO AID YOU ON THIS LITTLE QUEST
> I HAVE A SPLENDID VIEW OF WEST
> I HIDE AWAY DEEP IN THE PAST
> WHERE THE RISING TIDE WILL REACH ME LAST.

'Hmm,' I mumbled, 'interesting, interesting.'

'Oh yeah, really interesting,' said Lukc, 'But what's it going on about?'

'Not sure Lukey. This sounds like one for Quents.'

'Well I hate to disappoint everyone,' said Quentin, 'I don't know. It's got me stumped.'

'Well let's work on it,' said Anna, rolling up the riddle

again and slipping it back into the bottle. We wandered back down the beach to camp, each replaying the words of the riddle over and over in our heads.

15 SEEDS OF SAFETY

We'd almost arrived back at camp when I suddenly stopped in my tracks. 'Feast,' I said out loud, 'whatever happened to the feast? That last riddle promised us the 'key to the feast' and I'd like to know where it is.'

'Perhaps we need to work out this next riddle first?' suggested Anna.

'No, I bet we've missed something,' I replied, turning around and heading back towards the tree. None of the others followed. I wasn't surprised. They still didn't have my passion for food.

As you've probably guessed the word 'feast' is one of my favourite words. For me it ranks highly along with the words 'steak', 'chips', 'chocolate', and 'strawberries'. It is, and I think you would agree, a noble word, which conjures up images of tables overflowing with exotic delicacies. So yes, I admit it and I lift up my hands. That five letter word did grab my attention more than just a little.

It is true that we weren't exactly going hungry. For a

start we managed to catch the occasional pig and we were demolishing enough bananas to give us severe 'banana belly', if there was such a complaint. We also ate coconuts and mangoes and a few other berries and nuts that we recognised. However, the point is, that on the island there was such a wonderful variety of *potential* food growing all around us, but we didn't dare eat it. We had learned from Anna's adventure with the berries, only to eat the fruits and nuts that we were sure were safe. To me this seemed an awful shame. It was a bit like being in a sweet shop, but only being allowed to try two or three of the sweets.

Despite having only just been to the tree that morning, I had great difficulty finding it again. By the time I eventually did, I was pretty fed up. It was almost lunchtime and I hadn't even eaten breakfast!

I stretched my fingers into the hole where Anna had found the bottle, and rummaged around. And there, right at the back of the hole I tapped something with a finger.

I was right, there was something else. Anna had missed it. I grabbed a stick from the ground and pushed it into the hole. Carefully I managed to nudge the object towards me and grab it between two fingers. I drew it out slowly and placed it on the sand in front of me. It was a small, flat tin; the type people used to keep tobacco in. Although it was pretty rusted, I managed to prize open the lid. Inside, to my surprise were a dozen or so different types of seed. Some were very small, others were larger. I then noticed some words carved on the inside of the metal lid. Although the rust made them hard to read, I managed to make out the words.

'Inside each seed is all the magic and all the instructions for another life.'

INSIDE EACH SEED IS ALL THE MAGIC AND ALL THE INSTRUCTIONS FOR ANOTHER LIFE

And underneath that, were four larger words:
'Follow the tree diagram.'

FOLLOW THE TREE DIAGRAM

But there was no tree diagram. I knew what a tree diagram was. It was a way of sorting different species of animals or plants, or anything really. Miss Dawson showed us how to use one. I looked all over the box to see if I'd missed it and then rummaged around again in the key hole. It wasn't there.

Then a thought struck me. 'What better place for a tree diagram than on a tree!' On a hunch, I walked around the tree and there, sure enough, on the back, carved beautifully into the trunk, was a splendid tree diagram that sorted the very seeds that I had in my hand.

'Brilliant,' I thought. If this was the '*key to a feast*', then this diagram was showing which seeds came from plants that were edible and which ones were not! Then, by checking the seeds of any new fruit or berries that we came across, we would know whether it was safe to eat them.

My attention was suddenly grabbed by one of the markings near the base of the tree, next to one of the carved seeds. It was the dreaded skull and cross bones! I wondered, might that be the seed from the berries that Anna had eaten? We would have to take great care working through the diagram, otherwise we might not be as lucky as Anna. However, with this new information, we would now be able to eat a wider variety of food available on the island!

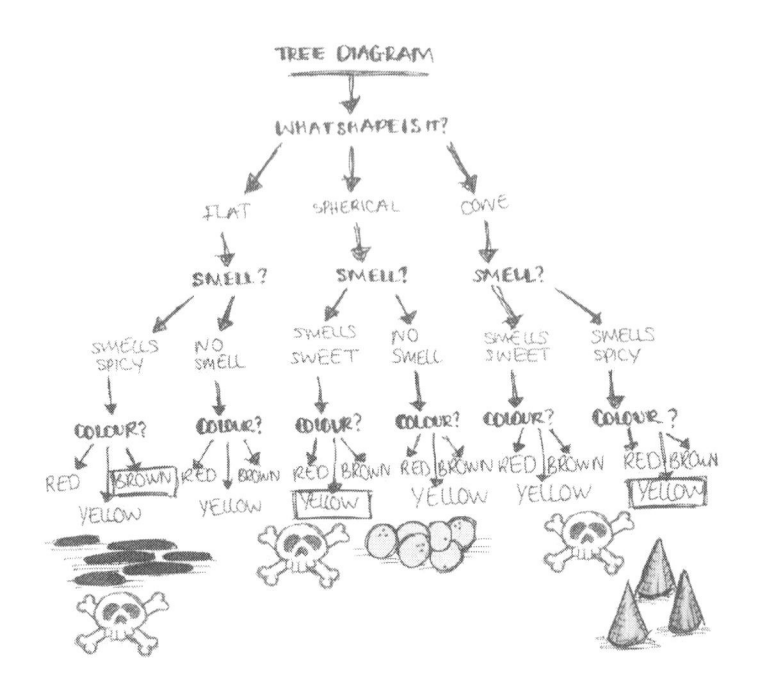

TREE DIAGRAM

WHAT SHAPE IS IT?

FLAT → SMELL?
- SMELLS SPICY → COLOUR? RED / **BROWN** / YELLOW ☠
- NO SMELL → COLOUR? RED / **BROWN** / YELLOW

SPHERICAL → SMELL?
- SMELLS SWEET → COLOUR? RED / BROWN / **YELLOW** ✓
- NO SMELL → COLOUR? RED / BROWN / YELLOW ☠

CONE → SMELL?
- SMELLS SWEET → COLOUR? RED / BROWN / YELLOW
- SMELLS SPICY → COLOUR? RED / BROWN / **YELLOW** ☠

And so it was, that the strange person, who we had now named 'The Rhymer', had helped us. In their bizarre way they had given us 'the key' to a wide variety of free food on the island. 'Bye bye banana-belly, bye bye.'

Several weeks later, the five of us were lazing around outside Number 1, Palm Trees Court. Although it was a fairly cool day by the island's standards, it was still very warm. It was also very quiet. As usual, there was no traffic noise, no noisy neighbours or police sirens. The only sound came from the waves breaking on the reef, the occasional whisper of the breeze through the palm leaves above us and the playful chatter of a pair of macaws playing a few feet away. They were the only sounds. And then suddenly they weren't.

'Magical mirrors,' cried out Quentin. The two macaws flew off terrified, 'I think I've got the first point of that riddle. Someone read it out again.' I went and fetched the riddle which we'd put with the other riddles in the shelter. Then I read it out for the hundredth time:

> 'Well done my friends, you're getting hot
> I knew you'd find the tree
> So now let's take another step
> With riddle number three.
>
> To solve this clue in one lifetime
> I must reflect along the line
> That travels from the south to north
> And there you'll find the precious fourth.
>
> …'

'Stop, that's enough,' butted in Quentin. 'Do you remember using mirrors in maths to reflect things?' We nodded, 'Well, things on one side of the mirror line, (the line of symmetry), are reflected to the same place on the other side of the line.' He bent down and began to draw in the sand with his finger. 'If the line is here, from south to north, we are just below here, he said, marking an X in the east, where we found the tree riddle.

'If you put a giant mirror along the line from south to north, this X would be reflected over here,' he explained, drawing another cross on the western side of the island,' and,' he continued, 'from there you would have a good view of the west!'

'I think you're right,' smiled Luke, 'and I think I've solved the second part too, listen. The riddle says '**The rising tide will reach me last**,' so it must be somewhere high up, you know, on the cliff. And, where it says it's '...**deep in the past**', I reckon it maybe in a hole. Because if you dig underground you find things from the past. That's my guess anyway.'

Later that evening we sat around our little campfire roasting bananas and some nuts that Anna had collected. For a change, although it was painful, we chatted about home; about our family, our friends and we tried to imagine what they would be doing just then. Would they be thinking of us tonight too?

The sand was cool underneath us and our beach looked beautiful in the light of the half moon. The stars above us shone majestically. Their patterns had become much more familiar to us now, since we'd been on the island. The sea breathed rhythmically on the shore below us, licking the sand softly with its frothy white tongue. From time to time we would see a shooting star leap across the heavens.

'Everybody knows that they're not really stars,' Anna had told us one night, 'but lumps of rock zipping around space that break through into our atmosphere. You see,' she had explained, 'the earth is surrounded by a layer of gases called 'the atmosphere'. It's a bit like the peel around an apple. When a rock zooms through this, it gets so hot because of friction that it burns up. And that's what you see - a falling lump of burning rock. Sometimes the rocks don't burn up completely and they land on Earth!'

I knew she was right because I'd seen one in a museum once with my Grandad. Mostly the bits of rock are pretty small, but I'd seen one on the internet which was as big as a car and weighed 66 tons! I wondered, perhaps Quentin's rock-magnet had come from space? You know, some people think that one day a gigantic meteor could even destroy planet Earth! But I still thought that shooting stars were beautiful.

We spent many nights like this, lying on our backs on the sand, staring upwards into the heavens. Some nights we would not say much, but just gaze upwards. It was so peaceful, so big. I often thought I could just reach up and touch the stars with my fingertips; they were so bright and they all seemed incredibly close. Sometimes Aisha might suggest playing 'dot to dot'. So one of us would make up patterns with the stars, like the ancients did. The rest of us would then try to guess what they were.

16 CAT - ASTROPHY

'Right,' said Aisha, early the next morning, 'let's have fodder time and set off as soon as we can.'

'Just a minute guys,' said Anna, 'when we get to the other side of the island, how will we know that we are right opposite to where the tree riddle was? We could easily wiggle all over the place as we walk across the island and end up miles off course.'

'Good point,' I said, 'we'll have to use Quentin's compass and walk directly west from the tree where we found the last riddle.'

'But that will take us directly over the middle of the island and right across the highest part of the rocky ridge. We'll never do that,' complained Anna.

'I don't think we have a choice,' said Luke calmly. 'Anyway, it might not be too bad.'

We soon set off. First for the tree where we'd found the riddle before turning inland and heading west. Quentin led the way, stopping now and then to check the direction with his compass. We pushed through thick jungle and then up, up we went towards the backbone of the island.

The mountains in front of us loomed larger and larger. As we drew nearer we could see their true height. They would take us hours, perhaps even a whole day to climb. We collapsed exhausted at the foot of an immense wall of rock that was blocking our path. It rose high in front of us like a mighty wave. There was no chance at all of getting over that. It was impossible to scale without proper climbing equipment.

'Great, what a waste of time,' sighed Quentin. 'We'll never get over that.'

'No we won't,' agreed Aisha, 'but if *Lukey Boy* used his eyes for once,' she said jokingly, 'he might just see what I can.'

'Well done Aisha, you beat me that time,' said Luke smiling too.'

'What are you two going on about?' I asked slightly frustrated.

'Look, over there!' We followed the direction of Aisha's nod and just caught sight of some rabbits squeezing themselves through a spiky, green bush. As I looked closer I could see that the bush was covering the entrance to a very narrow, stony path. It seemed to cut straight through between the rocks.

'I bet you that leads right through the mountains,' said Aisha, as she set off and squeezed herself carefully through the spiky bush. The rest of us followed. Sure enough the path wound itself neatly between two great walls of rock. Like Moses through the Red Sea, Aisha led us along the narrow winding path. At some points it was so narrow that it was difficult to squeeze through, but as we continued it broadened out into more of a path.

I was at the back daydreaming and thinking just how much time the path was saving us, when suddenly something made me turn around. There on the path behind me, perhaps only three metres away, I saw it. Two piercing round eyes stared at me. Two sharply pointed ears, large whiskers and a hard, cruel mouth overflowing with razor-like teeth. It was a cat, but not the cuddly armchair variety. This was a wild cat; the size of a large dog. It stood there glaring at me. I knew what it was thinking. It was thinking, 'I'm going to eat you.' It purred, 'Grrrrrrr' and the others spun around too. It took a pace towards us and we took a pace backwards. Again it moved forward and seemed to lick its lips. It looked hungry. 'Don't look scared,' I told myself and 'no sudden movements.' I backed off slowly, edging away from our unwelcome companion.

'Keep still,' whispered Anna into my ear. 'Don't move.' I then felt her hand in my rucksack searching for something. Next I saw a large hunk of pork that I had brought for our lunch, fly past me and land on the path in front of the wild cat. She sniffed it once, then grabbing it with both paws she arched her back and began to tear at it wildly with those teeth.

We didn't hang around to watch. We crept slowly backwards for several metres and then we turned and ran. We ran non-stop, all the way to the grassy cliffs on the western side of the island. There we slumped to the ground exhausted and rolled over on to our backs, sucking in precious mouthfuls of oxygen. I could feel my heart thundering away like never before – pumping – pumping – pumping. I put my fingers to my neck and to my wrist. I could clearly feel the thud of my pulse as blood squeezed through narrow tunnels of arteries; bashing, bashing against their walls. My blood was being pumped to every corner of my body and feeding it with the oxygen and the food that it craved. I thought for a moment about shouting out in a loud voice 'Thank you blood', but then I thought the others would think I was a little weird; so I decided to keep quiet. I looked up at the puffy white clouds that dotted the sky above us and breathed heavily - in and out.

17 OVER THE EDGE

We must have remained there a good half an hour. No-one wanted to move. Eventually I did and that was only because I was hungry. I pulled out some fruit from my rucksack and passed it around. We ate.

'Let's find that hole,' said Anna finally and we split up and began to comb the area like detectives going over a crime scene.

'There's nothing here,' shouted Luke after a long search. 'Perhaps I was wrong about the hole. Aisha, you've got the riddle, read out the second part again.' Aisha cleared her throat and did as Luke requested.

'To aid you on this little quest
I have a splendid view of west
I hide away deep in the past
Where the rising tide will reach me last.'

> TO AID YOU ON THIS LITTLE QUEST
> I HAVE A SPLENDID VIEW OF WEST
> I HIDE AWAY DEEP IN THE PAST
> WHERE THE RISING TIDE WILL REACH ME LAST.

'Oh no,' groaned Anna suddenly. 'I'm sure I've got it. Luke, I think you were almost right. It's like a hole, but not quite. From a hole you wouldn't have a good view of the west would you, but…from the cliff-face…' she said, peering sheepishly over the edge of the cliff, 'you would have the best view of all.'

We looked at each other and then, very, very tentatively, each lay down and bent over the edge of the cliff. Below us, way down, the sea smashed angrily against jagged rocks. Clouds of spray spat into the air. Even from where we were, high up on the cliff edge, the noise of the waves crashing was loud. So too was the deep sucking, gurgling sound, as they were pulled violently back again through the rocks.

We lay flat on our fronts. It felt safer that way, but not safe. Nervously we scanned the cliff face below us for anything unusual. The rock was not a single colour. It was many shades of grey and brown which made a striped pattern like in a Mars Bar after you've had a bite. Each different coloured layer was a different age. The lower you went down, the older the rock was.

'There!' indicated Luke. We followed his eyes downward and there, about two metres below us and over to our left, was a small nook in the rock.

'Well, if that's it we might as well give up!' I said, standing up and walking away.

'No way, we're not giving up,' said Anna sternly. 'Pass

me the bag.' She grabbed the rucksack, took out the rope inside and tied it around her waist. 'Right, my go,' she said, 'don't drop me. *Now*, before I change my mind!'

'You're crazy,' laughed Aisha as she took hold of the rope. The rest of us joined her. We all grabbed the rope, but said nothing. Anna then lay down on her front, swivelled around and carefully lowered herself, feet first, over the cliff edge. The rest of us stood back from the edge and let out the rope inch by inch, holding on to it for all we were worth. Terrified, we watched, as Anna's head disappeared slowly from our view.

'A bit lower,' called up Anna. 'Just a few more centimetres.' Just then the wind picked up and tried to knock us off balance. We stood firm for our friend.

'Come on Anna, forget it. It's not worth it,' shouted Quentin.

'Just give me a minute,' replied Anna. 'Okay, beam me up Scottie,' she called back.

Slowly and firmly we pulled up the rope, muscles strained to their limit. And soon Anna was standing safely beside us once again on the cliff top. We all hugged her and congratulated her on being so brave.

'Don't worry,' said Quentin, 'It doesn't matter.'

'What do you mean it doesn't matter,' replied Anna as she produced a small wooden box that she had tucked under her arm. 'This,' she said, 'was nestled inside the hole, with a good view of the west! I only just managed to reach it. Now stop fussing. Here we go,' she said, as she knelt down with the box and slid her fingers under a small metal latch. The box opened easily and revealed as we were expecting, another scrappy piece of leaf-paper. Anna reached in and pulled it out. She unfurled it and then began to read.

'Well good for you my future friends
I hope you like the view
So now we move to number four
The vital, final clue.

I'm still alive, but that you know
From reading number two
Yet old, as old as land itself
And getting in a stew!

When finally my wrath explodes
And pours out on this land
No man nor beast, nor even tree
Before my path will stand.

Where North meets South and East meets West
It's easy now I've said
But if you're really *still* not sure
'The centre for the dead!'

P.S.
Now please, be brave, don't be afraid
I've lived my dream you know
I am now old, but I'm at home
And hope I've helped you grow.'

> WELL GOOD FOR YOU MY FUTURE FRIENDS
> I HOPE YOU LIKE THE VIEW
> SO NOW WE MOVE TO NUMBER FOUR
> THE FINAL, VITAL CLUE.
>
> I'M STILL ALIVE, BUT THAT YOU KNOW
> FROM READING NUMBER TWO
> YET OLD, AS OLD AS LAND ITSELF
> AND GETTING IN A STEW!
>
> WHEN FINALLY MY WRATH EXPLODES
> AND POURS OUT ON THIS LAND
> NO MAN NOR BEAST, NOR EVEN TREE
> BEFORE MY PATH WILL STAND
>
> WHERE NORTH MEETS SOUTH AND EAST MEETS WEST
> IT'S EASY NOW I'VE SAID
> BUT IF YOU'RE REALLY STILL NOT SURE
> 'THE CENTRE FOR THE DEAD!'
>
> PS.
>
> NOW PLEASE, BE BRAVE, DON'T BE AFRAID
> I'VE LIVED MY DREAM YOU KNOW
> I AM NOW OLD, BUT I'M AT HOME
> AND HOPE I'VE HELPED YOU GROW.

We were too tired to think about the riddle just then, even if it was 'easy'. We packed our things together and set off wearily to base camp. This time we went around the bottom of the island. Although this way would take us longer, we knew it well. We were not in the mood to meet any hungry, wild cat. We were hungry and wanted supper, but we didn't want to *be* supper!

When we arrived back, we were exhausted. We

appreciated 'Number 1, Palm Trees Court' even more now that we knew that there were dangerous animals on the island. After supper we lit a small fire and stayed up chatting for a while. In the trees behind us a mass of birds was noisily gathering together. They flitted from perch to perch, restlessly, as they welcomed their friends.

We roasted bananas over the fire and watched it spit sparks every time banana juice dripped into the flames. We watched the dark wood slowly change into a powdery white ash, as its energy turned into heat energy and floated magically away, upwards towards the stars. Way up above us, we watched a great cloud of birds fly off across the sea.

'I'm really missing home,' I sniffled, trying to hold back the tears.

'Me too,' said Luke. 'Do you think we will ever get back? Do you think anyone is still bothering to look for us?'

'I don't know Luke, but we can't give up. We must never give up.'

Just then a warm breeze blew from the sea, and the embers around the fire glowed a deep orange colour. We sat there gazing at the flames. The wood that was being turned into charcoal and ash could never turn back into wood. We too had changed. We could never be the same again after this adventure...that is, if there was an 'after'.

As we drifted off to sleep, I thought I heard another large cluster of birds fly off over the sea.

18 DREAM OF THE RED JELLY BABY

None of us slept peacefully that night. We all had nasty dreams thanks to that riddle; of dragons, of fire and destruction and all sorts of scary things. I awoke screaming in terror, just as I was being pushed into a stew of Brussels sprouts and cabbage by my little brother! I could still hear his laughter as I began slowly to realise it had been a dream.

They're strange aren't they dreams. They're sort of real, but then, they're not. Things we see or hear about during the daytime often turn up in our dreams somehow. However, usually the details are all wrong. For example, a tiny red jelly-baby that you've eaten during the day comes back in your dream as a giant red 'child-eater' and gobbles you up in revenge! And come to think of it, I don't have a little brother. I have a little sister!

Where do dreams come from I wondered? But I had no time to wonder, because all of a sudden there was a mighty growl which shook the whole island. The hairs on my arms and legs stood dancing on their ends and we all jumped up ready to run. But we didn't know where to run.

A second time, another mighty growl thundered around us.

'It's the volcano, it must exist,' quivered Quentin. 'It's getting angry...it's waking up.'

We stood there frozen to the spot for ages. We were terrified, but unable to react. What could we do? Where could we go? There really wasn't anything that we could do except run into the sea, swim a bit and then drown. However ten minutes went by and there were no more growls. In fact, there were no more growls that morning at all.

'Perhaps they had just been yawns. Perhaps this volcano was a friendly volcano. Perhaps it was still fast asleep, in the middle of a scary dream itself,' I thought.

'Okay,' said Aisha calmly, after some time. 'We must find whatever it is that the riddles are leading us to. I have a hunch that whatever it is, it will help us get off this horrible island.'

She rolled out the fourth riddle again and we gathered around her. Once again she read it out slowly.

'Well we now know this volcano exists,' said Anna.

'Yeah and I know where it is,' declared Quentin. 'The Rhymer' was right; it is easy. 'Where north meets south and east meets west', that must be in the middle. It matches up with this bit look,' he added, reading from the fourth verse, '**The centre for the dead!**' 'Where is the centre for the dead?'

'The dead centre,' we all chimed in at once. Yes of course, that was obvious!

'But surely, we would have seen it yesterday on the path when we cut across the middle of the island,' said Luke.

'No,' I retorted, 'remember when we were running

from the wild cat? We weren't looking at anything. We were just running.'

'And actually,' said Quentin, 'thinking about it, didn't the path kind of wind around in a curve. I'm sure it wasn't straight.'

'Yes, now you mention it Quentin,' I said, joining in, 'I think it did. Maybe we ran right around it and didn't notice!'

We all agreed that although it was hard to tell where the roar of the volcano had come from, as it seemed to come from everywhere, it was very likely that it had indeed been from the middle of the island.

'So that's it,' said Anna. 'There lies our 'key to the mysteries of the universe' and probably our way off this island. It's near to an angry volcano and a vicious, wild cat – just perfect.'

'The thing is, we really don't have much of a choice,' stated Luke with a sigh. 'Well actually we've got two choices. One, we do nothing and wait for that thing to erupt and cover us with tomato soup. Two, we face the wild cat and the volcano, go after this key, and hopefully find a way off this island.'

'Yeah, come on,' said Aisha brightly. 'Luke is right. We have two choices, but only one is worth choosing.'

'What about the wild cat?' I asked. 'If there is one, there's bound to be others you know.'

'Well,' replied Aisha, 'as Anna said, the second choice is not worth choosing. We've got to go for it, we've got to find that key. And I suggest we don't waste any more time either.'

'Let's find some weapons in case we meet the cat again or its family,' said Anna wisely. 'And let's take that last bit of pork!' she added. 'Oh and let's leave as soon as we can.'

Before long, for the second time in two days, we were pacing inland towards the centre of the island. We took the same route as we had the day before, weaving our way through the jungle and trying to retrace our steps. Suddenly we became aware of a strange noise, a rustling sound that we had not heard before. The rustling grew louder and louder and seemed to be coming from every direction. It seemed to be coming from the ground itself!

'What is it?' I yelled, 'What is that?' Quentin gave the answer.

'Errrrr...rodents!' he shrieked. And he didn't mean dents in the road either. The jungle floor below us was now alive with dozens of rats and mice scurrying this way and that through the undergrowth. No, not dozens, there were hundreds, maybe thousands of them! The whole ground was a writhing tide of brown fur, legs and whiskers. It was like rat rush hour!

'They know,' said Luke amazed.

'Know what Lukey?' asked Aisha, in a concerned voice.

'Remember what 'The Rhymer' told us? He said that the animals would know when the volcano was about to erupt. Look at them. I don't think I've seen a single rat until today...and now look, they're everywhere! And remember last night?' he said, looking at me. 'The birds, they were leaving the island.'

'Oh no,' I groaned, 'Luke's right. I don't think we've got much time. We must get on.'

We pressed on through the sea of rats and mice that tumbled over our feet and ankles like a flood. We tried to 'tread air' but gravity wouldn't let us do that. Soon however, the rats and mice thinned and before long they had disappeared altogether. In no time it seemed, we arrived at the foot of the mountains and 'Wild Cat Alley', as we had named it. Cautiously, with white knuckles gripping firmly to the sticks we'd brought with us, we pushed past the spiky bush and filed swiftly along the stony path we had discovered the previous day. This time our eyes were peeled and alert for every movement. We noticed every shrub on the path, every rock and every crevice. Several times one of us froze and the rest of us copied them, thinking they had heard or seen something. And for quite some time we continued this strange game of musical statues.

We hadn't spoken a word for some time when Quentin broke the silence. 'Look!' he whispered excitedly, 'The path is curving around to the right just as we said.'

But there was no volcano here, or as far as the eye could see. The rocks that the path was bending around were only a few metres high. We could easily see right over them. There was definitely no volcano on the other side. We could see all around us. We must have got the riddle wrong. The volcano wasn't here.

But at that very moment, as if our thoughts had been read, came a noise so deafening, so deep, so terrifying and so very, very close, that we dropped like bullets to the shaking ground. As we dropped to the ground, we covered our ears, shut our eyes and screamed. I was convinced that the most enormous monster was about to devour us...and I waited for my end to come. The roar rumbled on for twenty to thirty seconds, enough time to realise that it was actually no animal, but a living monster of a very different kind. It was of course the volcano! This was the same growl that we had heard earlier that day, but this time, the noise was something else. For we must have been just feet away from the volcano's mighty mouth after all.

When the noise eventually came to an end, we all

scrambled up over to the rocks on the side of the path. We peered over and were greeted by the huge black opening of the volcano itself! We had been walking just feet from its edge and hadn't even realised. We had all been looking for a pointed volcano, sticking up clearly in a cone shape like you see on T.V. However, although this volcano was huge, it was only slightly higher than the surrounding mountains. That's why we had not spotted it before; because it had just looked part of the mountain range.

From the edge of the volcano we looked down with awe into the vast cavernous mouth below us. Even if we could have spoken, there was nothing to say. We then swiftly scanned the area and began our search for the key. We had no time to lose. We soon forgot about the rats and the wild cats. Compared to this huge beast of nature that we were standing on, they were 'child's play'. In any case, the cats had probably fled like the other animals.

Our challenge was where to start looking for the key. The circumference of the volcano was huge, so there were almost endless places it could be.

'I reckon it's about a quarter of a mile all the way around,' said Quentin. 'But that's an estimate.'

'Well now you can estimate where the key is Quentin!' said Anna, half joking, half annoyed.

'I can't estimate that, Anna,' he said, not realising she was only mucking around. 'I can only guess at that, but that's different.'

Anna smiled. 'Yes Quentin,' she said, 'Get guessing then!'

'Whilst you lot are chatting,' said Anna in her teacher's voice, 'Luke and I will go and search this way.' And off they marched to the left. Aisha, Quentin and I took the hint and went off to the right. We didn't really know what we were looking for - just something unusual we supposed. The riddle wasn't very specific. It had simply guided us to the volcano. The problem was, 'The Rhymer' could not have known that the volcano would be coming alive at the very moment we were searching for the key...could they? There was now an almost constant plume of dark smoke rising from the mouth of the volcano. We all knew that it could erupt at any moment and that would be that – 'goodbye World'. But if we focused on that, we knew we wouldn't be able to search properly for the key. Inside I was petrified, we all were. But we pushed it to the back of our minds and tried hard to concentrate on the task before us.

The rim of the crater wasn't particularly narrow. It was about a metre or so wide, but it was very uneven and covered in loose rocks and shingle. It then fell away steeply for several more metres, before ending abruptly. Each time I peered over the edge and into the blackness beside me, my stomach churned and I felt like I was going to be sick.

Then suddenly I spotted what we were looking for. 'Here, here it is!' I yelled and beckoned the others over to where I was standing. 'There, see that?' I pointed over the edge of the crater to a large rock several metres away. Around it was tied a thick rope which snaked around the edge of the rock and then dangled down into the heart of volcano itself!

'Typical!!' blurted out Aisha, 'This had better be worth it!' Her voice gave away the fear we all shared. One of us would have to go down, and time...well... we didn't know how much time we had left.

Before we could argue with her, Aisha was clambering over the edge and making her way cautiously towards the rock. She took hold of the rope and pulled it up towards her. It was long, about twenty to thirty metres. Aisha tied it tightly around her waist and then began easing herself slowly down into the mouth of the volcano. 'Come and hold the rope here,' she called back to us, 'I'll tug it twice when I want to come up. You'll have to pull me out.' Aisha's head then disappeared from our view as she eased herself down.

The rest of us scrambled nervously down to the rock. We took hold of the rope so we would feel when Aisha tugged at it. Anxiously we peered over the edge and into the volcano and could now see Aisha lowering herself inch by inch. Down, down she went until it was hard to make her out against the blackness.

Then suddenly the four of us were hurled violently backwards as the volcano gave out another deafening roar.

'Aisha,' we screamed. 'Aisha!'

The roar continued for another half a minute and thicker clouds of smoke wafted out from its insides.

'Aisha,' we yelled again. 'Aisha!!!!' We stared down at the dangling rope in front of us. Our eyes followed it down and down, but there was no Aisha to be seen. I gave the rope a tug, but it was completely slack. 'Aisha, Aisha!!!!!!!!!!!!' Our voices echoed through and around the insides of the beast, like in a gigantic megaphone. 'Aisha,' I sobbed, 'poor thing.'

'I'm alright,' came a faint voice from below us. 'I'm alright.'

'Aisha, you're alive!' I yelled, still sobbing.

'There's a cave in the rock,' she called back. 'I clambered into it and untied the rope. I'm okay, a bit deaf, but still here. You can't get rid of me that easily!'

In a flash I decided to join her. I began shinning my way down the rope and soon I had joined Aisha in the cave.

'Thought you could do with the company,' I grinned, as my feet touched the floor of the most unusual place I'd ever been in. I was now standing in a cave, on the inside of a volcano. Below me there was blackness. Above me, there was blue sky and smoke. It was by no means a large cave. In fact, it was more of a large ledge than a cave. But whatever it was it had saved Aisha's life.

And there he was, 'The Rhymer', sitting up in the corner. He had big, round, dark eyes and was sporting a broad and toothy grin. In his hands he held a small wooden box, almost as if he was offering it to us. He had been dead a long, long time. His clothes hung loosely on his fragile frame and around his neck hung a gold chain with a cross on it. There was nothing else to be found. He didn't scare me. How could he? All I felt was sadness. Although we had never met him, he was in a funny way our friend and the sixth member of our group. I took the wooden box, whilst Aisha was being pulled up. Then, tucking the box under one arm, I gave two tugs on the rope which had been dropped back down, to signal that I too was ready.

'Let's get away from this thing,' said Luke, as soon as I reached him and the others, 'before it burps again.'

'We'll open the box back at camp,' I said, patting the lid gently. At last we had the 'key to the mysteries of the universe' as well as the key to getting off our island prison. So you can imagine, we almost flew back to camp!

19 THE MYSTERIES OF THE UNIVERSE

The box was small and beautifully crafted in dark, grainy wood, smoothed to perfection. Two brass hinges and a clasp firmly attached a lid decorated by 'Mother-of-Pearl' shell. Anna's fingers clicked the clasp undone and then she slowly began to raise the lid. Ten eyes stared intently and five mouths held their breath.

There was however no flash of lightning. There was no glowing key and no genie appeared suddenly to grant us each a wish. Instead, we found a small, white, cotton drawstring bag, which Anna withdrew immediately and began to loosen. Next her fingers reached into the bag and pulled out a rather small, bronze bracelet. It looked somewhat familiar.

Luke peered into the box to check if Anna had missed anything. 'That's all there is,' he said disappointed. 'There's nothing else there.'

'Wait a minute, look, there's something engraved on it,' remarked Anna, examining the bracelet more carefully. Indeed, around the outside of the bracelet, in beautiful, elegant writing, read the words: **'The mysteries of the universe lie hidden within'**.

'What does it mean, 'lie hidden within?" I asked.

'Look there, inside it,' said Luke, 'there's some more writing on the inside of it. Read it out Anna,' he said, leaning over the bracelet.

'I will if you move out of my light,' Anna replied, rather impatiently. Luke moved back to give Anna some space. Then, turning the bracelet carefully between her fingers, Anna read out the tiny words on the inside edge of the bracelet. She chose her own starting point, as there was no punctuation. It seemed it didn't matter where you started.

courage determination trust hope perseverance friendship kindness imagination love

'What's that all about?' I asked. 'Where's the key to the mysteries of the universe? How does that help us get off this island?' I looked at the others. We were all thinking the same thing. 'Was that it? Had we missed anything? Was that all there was? Had it all been a wild goose chase?'

'Fantastic,' said Luke sarcastically. 'All that effort, all that searching…for what, for an old stupid, useless bracelet?'

'I almost died getting that,' chimed in Aisha.

'Me too,' said Anna.

'I don't believe it,' I said, beginning to feel sick, confused, angry and frustrated all at once.

'This can't be true!' shouted Aisha, punching a fist into her other hand. 'All that for nothing! I hate him, even if he is dead,' she snapped, kicking the sand in anger. She then grabbed the bracelet off Anna and flung it furiously into the sand in front of us. The rest of us said nothing. We all felt the same. She had thrown the bracelet away for all of us.

Just then came another long rumble from the volcano. It reminded us – not that we needed reminding - of our situation. We had to get off the island and fast. But our hope that we had put on the riddles and the 'key to the mysteries of the universe', had now been smashed into pieces. All our efforts had come to nothing.

Again the volcano roared. The frequency of the roars was increasing now for sure. And each rumble seemed louder than the one before.

Then Anna, calm as ever, stood up and addressed us. She spoke each word slowly, thinking carefully through what she was trying to say.

'Let's not panic,' she began, 'listen, what if 'The Rhymer' knew more than we had thought? What if he knew we would be here today on this beach? What if he knew that the volcano would be coming alive at this precise moment? Could he have? Perhaps the 'key to the mysteries of the universe' are not just the words written within the bracelet. Perhaps 'The Rhymer' meant that the key, or 'keys to the mysteries of the universe', were within us?' There was a brief silence before the volcano sounded once again, as if congratulating Anna on her little speech.

'Maybe Anna, maybe...who knows,' said Quentin, trying not to deflate her speech. 'Look, the only thing I can think of doing is this. We make a raft – quickly. Just a flat raft. We load it with as much food as we can. Then before the volcano starts to explode we get paddling and hope for the best...what else can we do?'

There really was nothing else we could do. We just had to get off the island! 'Listen,' said Luke, 'We don't have time to cut all the wood up, so let's use the wood from the camp. If we lay out the wood flat, we've practically got a raft already. The wood is already tied together. We can just make a few quick adjustments and cover it with the tarpaulin.'

'You're right,' said Quentin. Let's do it. Let's go.' And off we went, like an army of ants under strict marching orders. We didn't need egging on either. The noises coming from the volcano were far better than any cheerleader.

It didn't take long before we had dismantled 'Number 1, Palm Trees Court' and had hashed together a makeshift raft. We had space for the five of us, (six including Boggo). We hastily crammed the food we had stored up, mainly bananas and some nuts, into two of the rucksacks. We included the small amount of pork we had left over that was covered with salt and wrapped in banana leaves to keep it from going off. The only water we had was four coconut shells full. We never stored much as it was something we collected every day.

As soon as we had finished, we carried our rickety craft across the sands and down to the water's edge. We now had to try it out. We pushed it carefully into the shallow water and then placed the two rucksacks on it. The raft bobbed up and down on the breakers as they rolled in, but it stayed afloat. When the waters reached our waists, we too clambered on, one by one. I scrambled on last and as I did, the waters rose up to within a few centimetres of the edge of the raft. A few centimetres is better than no centimetres at all. We were still floating.

Her maiden voyage over, we left the raft tied to a rock at the water's edge. This is where it would remain until we had no choice but to flee the island. We then trudged back up the beach exhausted and crashed out on the cool sand by the remains of our camp. It was now almost dark and the first stars were appearing. One minute they were not there, then suddenly 'ping', there they were. We each lay silently with our own thoughts. I looked back at the raft. 'What was the point?' I thought to myself, 'it might save us from the volcano, but then what? It wouldn't last long. Even if it did, we'd die anyway, slowly and painfully, as we ran out of water.'

20 THOUGHTS AND CROSSES

I looked down and noticed the bracelet. It was half-eaten by the sand where Aisha had flung it. I forced myself to my feet, took the few steps over to it and bent down to pick it up. I brushed off the sand and rolled it over in my fingers. Then slipping it on my wrist, I gazed upwards into the sea of black above. Tonight the stars appeared bigger and more beautiful than ever. We however felt let down and betrayed. We had finished the strange trail that we had hoped would lead us off the island along with the 'mysteries of the whole universe'. But the only mystery that remained, was how to escape, before a river of hot molten larva turned us into statues for a museum.

A million questions rolled around in the universe of my head. I found myself gazing up at the mighty Southern Cross; the constellation that was directly above us. That reminded me of the gold cross that *he* was wearing. Then suddenly my eyes picked up on a tiny faint dot, gliding steadily across the sky. It was way, way up and barely visible. It was a satellite. It was probably beaming down television programmes, or taking photographs for the weather forecast I imagined. 'Satellite', my mind repeated, 'satellite'… 'set-a-light'.

And then suddenly something clicked inside of me. In a flash I was racing up the beach and grabbing my map of the island. In the pale light of the moon I could scarcely read it. I quickly marked down the locations where we had found the riddles. First there was the riddle we found in the cave, to the south of the mountain ridge. Then the clue in the boat, up in the north. The next one we found in the tree on the eastern side of the island and then the fourth in the cliff in the west. Finally I marked the spot where we found the bracelet itself, in the volcano in the centre of the island. 'Eureka!' I whispered to myself, thumping the ground with my fist. 'X marks the spot!' I shouted. I was right. The five marks made a perfect cross. My brain raced. A satellite passing overhead would see a perfect cross. That is, if somehow the points were lit up together. Surely someone would notice that and would check it out? I dashed back to the others who were still sitting around glumly.

'Ladies and gentlemen, I think I've got it. It's mad but it might work.' I knelt down beside them with the map in front of me. 'Look, here is where we found the riddles. The first one was here behind the waterfall. Then we found the one in the boat over here. 'Anna's door' in the tree is here and the riddle in the cliff was here, opposite. And then, this is where we found the bracelet, here in the volcano, slap bang in the middle. Look, can you see, they make the shape of a cross!' I said. 'There are satellites right? Hundreds of them up there. I just saw one right overhead. If we 'set-a-light' each of these points.' The others nodded. They had got the idea.

'Eureka, you stinker, you ponger.' They all joked,

suddenly upbeat again.

The task before us was huge. We could never have done it at the beginning, when we were five frightened school children. But now we had grown up. Like a caterpillar which turns into a chrysalis and then into a butterfly, we had changed, each one of us. Our chrysalis was our island prison. We had learned and discovered many things in our prison. For one thing, we were now experts at lighting fires! Deep down within us, we all knew the bracelet told the truth. The mysteries of the universe were now in each of us and we were ready to fly!

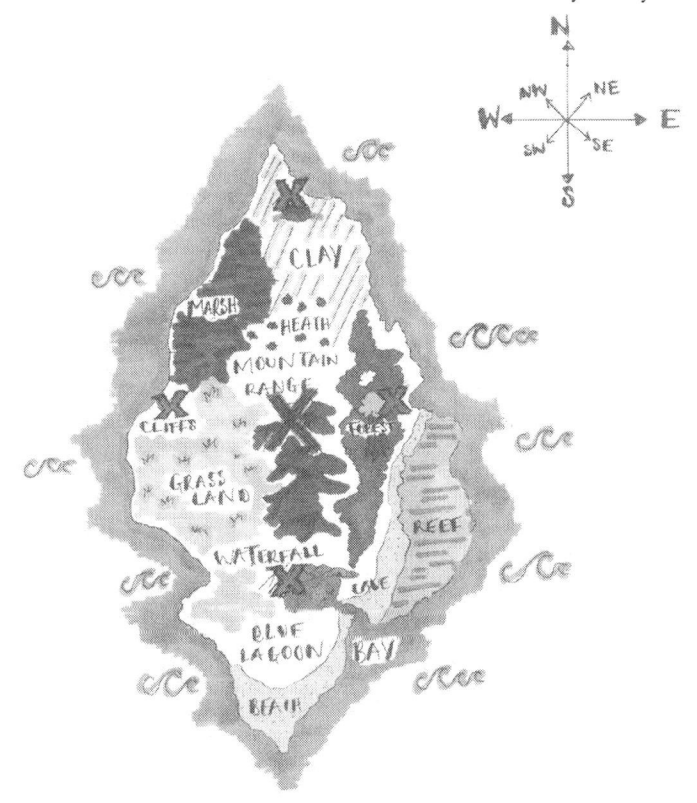

We would leave now. Each of us, to one of the five sites, on our own, in the dark. We would work non-stop throughout the night and throughout the next day. We would get cutting, tearing down, dragging and piling up as large a pile of firewood as we each could manage. We had until dusk the following evening. Then when the first stars appeared, that would be the sign for each of us to light our fire and make our way back swiftly to base.

Immediately we grabbed all the flints and cutting stones that we had collected and set off alone to our designated site. The moon alone lit our paths. We had no time to lose.

I don't wish to write about that night. Each of us has our own story that we have kept secret. It wouldn't be right to tell just mine. All I'll say, is that night, we overcame fears and dangers that we had once thought were impossible to conquer.

By dawn, my bonfire near 'Anna's Door' had really taken shape. We had each drawn straws to decide which site we would have. I guess I had been the luckiest. 'Anna's Door' was the closest and by far the safest of the five locations. So I'd made up my mind to work extra hard on my fire and then go and help Quentin out at the volcano site. He had been really brave. He had pulled out the volcano straw, but he hadn't moaned about it. Instead he had got straight on with it and what he knew he had to do.

By mid-morning I was exhausted and hungry. But I knew I had to keep going. We were all trusting each other to do a good job and I was not going to let anyone down. Just then the volcano, which had been quiet for several hours, let out an almighty bellow and snorted an enormous column of smoke into the air, like a mighty whale shooting spray skywards.

'Quentin,' I whispered to myself, 'Quentin…'

I forced myself to think of something else. I couldn't bear to think of my friend in danger. My mind flicked back to a geography lesson we once had with Miss Dawson. I remember she had drawn two pictures on the board.

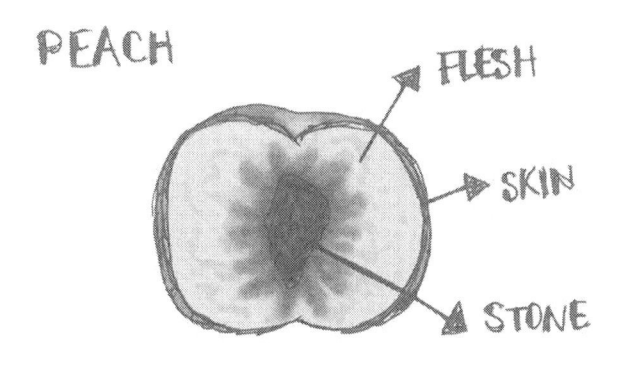

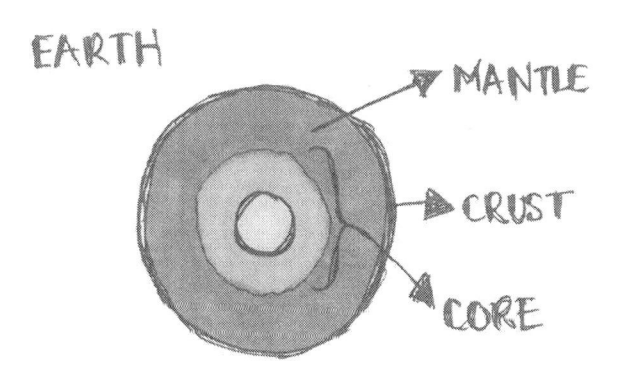

PEACH — FLESH, SKIN, STONE

EARTH — MANTLE, CRUST, CORE

One was of the inside of the Earth and one of the inside of a peach. 'Right in the centre of the Earth is the core,' she had explained, 'there's an inner core, which is solid and an outer core which is liquid. The inner core is like the stone in a peach. Around the core is the mantle, which is like the peach flesh and around the mantle, is the crust – like the skin of the peach.' She then told us that the core was made up of iron and nickel metals and what's amazing, I remember her saying, is that it is as hot as the surface of the sun - about 6000 °C!

Next, Miss Dawson told us all about magma. She said it was molten rock and it was stored under the surface of the Earth in chambers and sometimes flowed through gaps in the rock, like rabbits moving through a giant rabbit warren.

I remember imagining some gooey substance wanting desperately to escape, like an angry child who has been locked in their room all day long. Then I remembered Miss Dawson had noticed Aisha sipping from a bottle of Coke at the back of the class. She had carried on talking as she walked over to Aisha's desk, picked up the bottle and began to shake it up and down violently. 'It's like a fizzy drink that has been shaken up,' she explained. And with that, she had loosened the cap. The Coke had shot up the bottle, pushed off the cap and had sprayed out all over Aisha, Miss Dawson and the classroom floor.

'BOOOO!!' I jumped out of my skin. I had been so caught up with what I was doing and thinking about the Coke episode, that I hadn't seen him come up behind me.

'Quentin are you all right? I was worried…I saw the smoke…and I thought…'

'Yeah I'm fine, though I wasn't able to build much of a fire. I'm sorry. It was too dangerous. The volcano, it's really about to blow. It's like a firework…and somebody has already lit the fuse!'

'I know, it doesn't look good. But thank goodness

you're alright Quentin. Look I'm finished here. You go and help Aisha down at the lagoon and I'll go and give Anna a hand up the 'boat site.' He agreed and we parted swiftly.

When I arrived at the 'boat site' I was impressed by the giant pile of sticks, branches and even small trees that Anna had assembled. However we both kept working at it until dusk fell. Then, and as soon as the first stars 'pinged' into the sky, we lit the monster bonfire and made our way back down along the shore, as fast as our weary bodies and minds would drag us. We stopped just the once to light the fire I had built at 'Anna's Door'.

We were greeted back at base by an anxious Quentin and Aisha. And there we waited for Luke to arrive back from the 'cliff site' on the west of the island.

21 WAITING FOR LUKE

We sat around the remains of 'Number 1, Palm Trees Court', willing Luke to arrive. We suddenly became aware of a strange, sickly smell wafting over us. 'Yuck, rotten eggs,' groaned Aisha. She was right. That's exactly what it smelled like, rotten eggs.

'It's the smoke from the volcano,' said Quentin. 'I smelled it earlier. It's a gas called 'Hydrogen Sulphide'. It's what they make stink bombs from!'

We looked up in the direction of the volcano and could see that it was now spewing smoke continually upwards in a dark plume. Thick, choking clouds tumbled and rolled into the night sky, before rippling out into silver streamers that danced across the milky full moon. It was both eerie and very beautiful.

'Come on Luke,' urged Aisha under her breath. 'Come on, it's time we had left. This is not the time to be late.'

Then, despite all its warnings the volcano had given us, the terrifying crack that came next, made our hearts crumble in terror. The noise thundered across the island and fountains of fire leapt out of the volcano. We stared helplessly as a sea of larva began pouring out of the crater and began its march of destruction down the mountain slopes. Ash and 'larva bombs' spat out in all directions, crashing into trees and bushes and igniting them instantly.

We watched in horror as the orange lake of molten rock spilled down through the tree layer towards us. Rock that had been locked away, out of reach in the depths of the Earth, was now free.

'Let's go!' came a tired cry from within the bushes behind us. And then he appeared, staggering out of the blackness and onto the sands beside us.

'Luke, you made it!' we cried and we threw our arms around him.

'And that time keeping,' said Aisha, 'definitely improved!'

Dragging a half-collapsed Luke with us, we made it down to the water's edge. We untied the rope and hauled ourselves and Luke, who was now barely conscious, up onto the raft. Then, grabbing the paddles, we thrust them into the water and began to row away from the shore.

Slowly, agonisingly slowly, we inched away from the shore. More powerful explosions now hurled out volcanic rock as far as the beach and into the waters around us. Fiery missiles hit the water in a hiss of fury and steam, some missing us by only metres. The lake of fire slid sinisterly on, trampling and flattening everything in its way.

We looked back to the shore and saw a river of red-hot larva snaking its way out through the trees and across the sands where we had been just moments earlier. It was only when it reached the sea that it finally met its match; but it wasn't without a fight. We watched, with front row seats, as two mighty forces of nature clashed in battle in a cloud of hissing steam. The cold sea stole the larva's energy, turning it into solid rock and changing the coastline in an instant. And the larva kept coming. Sacrificing itself to the sea, but gaining ground, inch by inch.

Clinging desperately to our little raft, we moved steadily away from the island, our home for so long, and out into a darkness unknown. When we finally reached what we believed to be a safe distance, we stopped rowing. We slumped together in a big bundle and looked back at the burning island. For twenty-four hours we had worked desperately on building the fires and I'd almost forgotten why we had built them. I then remembered with clarity – rescue! Had we done enough? Were the fires large enough? Would our signal be spotted? Although Quentin had been unable to build much of a fire, the erupting volcano itself would have certainly completed the middle point of the cross.

Our little craft bobbed up and down with every tiny wave. 'Now what?' I said under my breath, as I felt sleep coming over me like a dark cloud. 'Now comes the end,' I thought.

I then felt the bracelet that I was still wearing. I tried to remember all the words written on it that now lay against my skin. **'Courage, determination, trust, hope'**…but I didn't have time to recall them all, as my weary mind gave way to the heavy, dark cloud of sleep.

Just then, or perhaps hours later, a harsh, bright, white light suddenly poured into my sleepy eyes. My mind was so confused by sleep, that I had no idea what was happening, or where I was.

'This is the U.S. Airforce,' came a loud voice over a thundering whir of helicopter blades. Next, through the white light, like an angel, came the first (live) human being that we had seen in many months. He lowered himself down to our raft, attached a harness around Anna and signalled back up to the helicopter. The two of them were then winched rapidly upwards. They disappeared into the white glare above, leaving behind four extremely dazed children. The angel soon appeared again and repeated his magic act three more times. I was then left all alone on the little wooden raft, in my own bright, island of light. I looked out into the darkness beyond and shivered. Then finally, he came down, one last time, and snatched me up upwards.

The helicopter then soared, turned sharply and we sped off into the night. At a distance, all that could be seen of the island was its glowing cross, still calling out to the world. We said barely anything. It all seemed like a dream. We knew we had been finally rescued, but it did not seem real. We had been saved, but we were all too tired and too stunned even to take it on board.

In under two hours we landed in the grounds of a large, modern hospital. A huge crowd of doctors, nurses and press photographers fussed around us as we were hustled inside to have a check-up. We then had a shower and were given pyjamas, a warm drink and a bed each to crash out on. It was very strange to have a bed with a pillow and sheets. It seemed far too comfortable to lie on. However, even that didn't prevent each of us from slipping immediately into deep, deep sleeps.

Morning came at about midday. Breakfast was in bed and unusual it was too. There were no bananas or mangoes or coconuts! Instead we had waffles with maple syrup, blueberry muffins, bagels and peanut butter, orange juice and hot-chocolate. It all tasted rather odd and we weren't sure about it at all. Perhaps we would grow to like it more?

As we were finishing our breakfasts, a nurse came into

our ward wearing a big smile on her face. 'I thought you might like to have a look at these,' she grinned, dropping a copy of the New York Times onto each of our beds.

'Oh thank you,' said Luke, 'thank you, thank you, thank you.' I picked up the paper in front of me and gawped as I read the front page.

'Dramatic rescue from 'Volcano Island'. Five School children Back from the Dead.'

DRAMATIC RESCUE FROM 'VOLCANO ISLAND'
FIVE SCHOOL CHILDREN BACK FROM THE DEAD

There were two main pictures. On the left was an aerial shot of the burning island, clearly showing the five glowing points of a cross. On the right was a photo of five bedraggled children from Firtrees Primary School, being led into hospital amid a frenzy of reporters and hospital staff.

'Wow!' cried Luke. 'Front page of the New York Times. Just wait until they see this at home.' The word 'home' hung frozen in the air, like a bird hovering overhead. We had tried mostly to forget about 'home' and had spoken very little about it since it was too painful. But now!!!

'I think it's time you spoke with your families,' said the nurse in a gentle voice, nodding to the screens besides our beds. 'You can Skype them now,' she said. I had almost forgotten that was possible, it had been so long.

Well I'm not going to share our private conversations that we had from our hospital beds, am I? But yes, they were very soppy, very tearful and very, very long.

Anyway, the next day we flew home first-class to Heathrow, London. There we were met by our families and of course, dozens of news crews and a host of reporters. It felt amazing walking silently through the middle of them, as if we were famous footballers returning from our overseas' triumph. All that 'news stuff' however, could wait until tomorrow. Today was for catching up with our families and friends.

22 SCHOOL REPORT

My dad arranged a press conference for the following evening down at the school. The five of us sat at a long table on the stage. Each of us had our own microphone, except Boggo, who Luke had placed proudly at the front of the table. All around the hall, lights and cameras were aimed at us. We looked out at a school-hall jammed full of people taking photographs, scribbling down notes and talking into mobile phones.

Mr. Carter then stood up to begin proceedings. 'Welcome,' he began. 'Welcome to Firtrees Primary School,' he continued. A small, but clearly visible smile, could then be seen creeping across Mr Carter's face. He paused and tried to compose himself. But this smile was alive. It was like an animal, caged for months that had just found its freedom. And I could see that Mr. Carter, who I had only once seen smile before, would not be able to contain this unshackled beast much longer. And within the space of two heartbeats, Mr. Carter had lost his little battle for composure. The smile quickly spread right across his leathery face like a forest fire. He gave up embarrassed and sat down.

Before he had even touched his seat, hands with questions at the end of them shot up from every inch of the hall. 'Thank you for inviting us,' began Luke politely. 'We will be delighted to answer all your questions. Let's first have the lady in row two,' he said, gesturing towards the female reporter from the local newspaper.

We then began taking turns to choose hands and to answer the million questions that the world wanted to know about us. 'How did we reach the island? What did we eat? What was the scariest part? Did we think we'd ever get home? Who is the small odd-looking purple guy with the big feet?'

When finally it was all over, we were invited into the staffroom to have drinks and nibbles with the teachers. And as we walked in, we were greeted by rapturous clapping and pats on the back.

'A toast,' said Mr. Carter cheerfully, relieved that once again his school was in the headlines for good reasons. 'A toast, to the five bravest children I've ever known.' He then raised his glass along with the other teachers and parents and siblings. 'To the five stars of Firtrees Primary School.'

'To the five stars of Firtrees Primary School,' they all chorused.

A tray of drinks and finger food was then brought around by the catering staff. The five of us piled our plates as high as we could, before splitting up to mix with the teachers and to chat with them about our adventures. After discussing the different species of animals that we had come across on the island with the head of Year Five, I went over to talk with Miss Dawson who was standing on her own in the corner of the room nearest to the biscuits!

'Hi Miss Dawson,' I said excitedly, stretching out my hand to shake hers. She took hold of my hand, shook it, but then did not let go. Instead she just kept staring at the bracelet on my arm. I then noticed it properly for the very first time. On her right hand, Miss Dawson wore an identical bronze bracelet. I had thought it had been familiar. I was right. I had seen the bracelet before, well, a similar one. It was the same size and shape and had exactly the same inscription on it to the one I was wearing; 'The mysteries of the universe lie hidden within'.

At last she released my tiring hand and looked me in the eyes, with one of those 'sad, but glad' looks. She then beckoned the others over to her and with tears glistening in her eyes, whispered to us gently, 'The Rhymer'...he was my father.' She paused, then continued slowly. 'My father was crazy about volcanoes, he had loved them since he was a young boy. When my mother died, he decided to sell the house and set off travelling around the world to study them. About fourteen years ago, I heard that he had been lost at sea somewhere, off the coast of Hawaii. I heard no more of him. Before he left, he had made these two bracelets. He gave this one to me and kept the other one himself. He promised me on the day he left, that I would one day wear them both, to remember my mother and him by.'

She wiped a tear with her finger. 'I think deep down I was angry that he had broken his promise. But now,' she smiled, as I passed her the second bracelet, 'now I know he wasn't lost at sea after all. Now I know he died doing what he loved and where he felt at home. Now that promise he made to me the last time I saw him, has come true.' She slipped the bracelet on her arm next to the one she was wearing. Then reached out and gave us all a big hug. 'Thank you,' she whispered. 'Thank you.'

'So be like the sun as it rises each day
Forgetting the clouds that were there yesterday.'

The End.

A planetpoetry® production

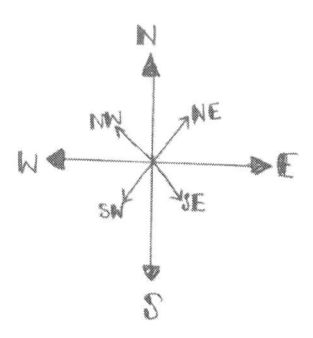

WWW.PLANETPOETRY.CO.UK

WWW.XIENTIFICA.COM